taste of home
COOKING
for TWO

spinach cheese soup, page 50

206 scrumptious recipes sized right for two!

Less is more when you use *Taste of Home Cooking for Two* to plan meals for a pair—more options...more flavor... more money left over in the grocery budget!

Created specifically for smaller households, *Cooking for Two* serves up 200+ perfectly portioned recipes for every meal and occasion. Page through the six tempting chapters to find your familiar staples, as well as new, exciting offerings you'll be eager to try.

Cooking for Two covers all the basics—breakfast, lunch and dinner—with an assortment of pleasing, pared-down fare such as Butter Pecan French Toast (p. 4), Cranberry Chicken Salad Sandwiches (p. 38) and Mushroom-Stuffed Chicken Breasts (p. 77).

Although the recipe yields in this book are reduced, the variety is huge! You'll find tasty selections for simmering soups, freshly baked breads, crisp salads and versatile side dishes. Round out a meal with Creamy Wild Rice Soup (p. 50), Mini Italian Herb Bread (p. 61), BLT Bread Salad (p. 69) or Creamy Baked Corn (p. 57).

Craving something sweet? The decadent selection of small-batch baking recipes in the Desserts chapter has you covered! Indulge in an assortment of scaled-back sweets such as Minty Baked Alaska (p. 93), Mini Apple Pie (p. 102) and Turtle Cheesecake (p. 105).

All 206 gotta-try, two-serving recipes are made using fresh and readily available ingredients and feature easy-to-follow instructions. We've even added mouthwatering photos and helpful cooking tips to ensure every recipe turns out great. With *Taste of Home Cooking for Two*, you'll say "good-bye" to leftovers and "hello" to never-ending mealtime possibilities!

taste of home.
COOKING for TWO

SENIOR VICE PRESIDENT, EDITOR IN CHIEF: Catherine Cassidy

VICE PRESIDENT, EXECUTIVE EDITOR/BOOKS: Heidi Reuter Lloyd

CREATIVE DIRECTOR: Howard Greenberg

FOOD DIRECTOR: Diane Werner RD

SENIOR EDITOR/BOOKS: Mark Hagen

EDITOR: Sara Lancaster

ART DIRECTOR: Rudy Krochalk

CONTENT PRODUCTION SUPERVISOR: Julie Wagner

PROJECT DESIGN LAYOUT ARTIST: Kathryn Pieters

PROOFREADER: Linne Bruskewitz

RECIPE ASSET SYSTEM MANAGER: Coleen Martin

PREMEDIA SUPERVISOR: Scott Berger

RECIPE TESTING AND EDITING: Taste of Home Test Kitchen

FOOD PHOTOGRAPHY: Taste of Home Photo Studio

ADMINISTRATIVE ASSISTANT: Barb Czysz

COVER PHOTOGRAPHER: Rob Hagen

COVER FOOD STYLIST: Alynna Malson

COVER SET STYLIST: Grace Natoli Sheldon

NORTH AMERICAN CHIEF MARKETING OFFICER: Lisa Karpinski

VICE PRESIDENT/BOOK MARKETING: Dan Fink

CREATIVE DIRECTOR/CREATIVE MARKETING: Jim Palmen

THE READER'S DIGEST ASSOCIATION, INC.

PRESIDENT AND CHIEF EXECUTIVE OFFICER: Mary G. Berner

PRESIDENT, NORTH AMERICAN AFFINITIES: Suzanne M. Grimes

INTERNATIONAL STANDARD BOOK NUMBER (10): 0-89821-842-X

INTERNATIONAL STANDARD BOOK NUMBER (13): 978-0-89821-842-8

LIBRARY OF CONGRESS CONTROL NUMBER: 2010938663

Printed in China
5 7 9 10 8 6 4

For other Taste of Home books and products,
visit ShopTasteofHome.com.

PICTURED ON COVER: INDIVIDUAL CHICKEN POTPIES, PAGE 78

table of contents

eggs lorraine, page 18

great gift! *Taste of Home Cooking for Two* makes a great gift for empty nesters, newlyweds and singles who still want to enjoy delicious, home-cooked meals, but not worry about large servings. To order additional copies, specify item number 41677 and send $14.99 (plus $4.95 shipping/ processing for one book, $5.95 for two or more) to: Shop Taste of Home, Suite 391, P.O. Box 26820, Lehigh Valley, PA 18002-6280. To order by credit card, call toll-free 1-800/880-3012.

breakfast & brunch

You don't have to invite a large group over to enjoy your favorite brunch fare. These pared-down traditions capture all the flavor without lengthy prep work or leftovers.

hearty breakfast combo, page 7

apple pancakes with cider syrup

cooking tip

The next time you make Apple Pancakes with Cider Syrup, use a whisk to mix up the batter. A whisk will blend the ingredients more thoroughly and quickly, reducing the risk of overmixing. This handy trick also works well when preparing your favorite waffle and muffin recipes.

April Harmon
Greeneville, Tennessee
These tender pancakes are filled with minced apple and raisins, and drizzled with apple cider syrup. They're wonderful in the summer or on a cool fall morning.

apple pancakes with cider syrup

1/2   cup all-purpose flour
1/4   cup whole wheat flour
  2   teaspoons sugar
1/4   teaspoon baking soda
1/4   teaspoon salt
1/4   teaspoon ground cinnamon
2/3   cup minced peeled apple
1/4   cup raisins
2/3   cup buttermilk
  1   egg, *separated*
  2   teaspoons butter, melted
1/4   teaspoon vanilla extract
SYRUP:
1/4   cup sugar
  2   teaspoons cornstarch
2/3   cup apple cider *or* juice

  1   cinnamon stick (1-1/2 inches)
Dash ground nutmeg
Additional butter, optional

In a small bowl, combine the first six ingredients; stir in apple and raisins. Combine the buttermilk, egg yolk, butter and vanilla; stir into dry ingredients. In a small bowl, beat egg white until soft peaks form; fold into batter.

Pour batter by heaping 1/4 cupfuls onto a hot griddle coated with cooking spray; turn when bubbles form on top. Cook until the second side is lightly browned.

Meanwhile, in a small saucepan, combine the sugar, cornstarch and cider until smooth; add cinnamon stick. Bring to a boil over medium heat; cook and stir for 2 minutes or until thickened. Discard cinnamon stick. Stir nutmeg into syrup. Serve pancakes with warm syrup and additional butter if desired. **yield: 6 pancakes (2/3 cup syrup).**

ham 'n' egg muffins

Emily Chaney • Blue Hill, Maine
Although this recipe stars traditional breakfast ingredients, it's a staple Saturday night supper at our house. We usually serve it with a salad and fruit. Sometimes, I double the recipe for brunch the next day.

- 1 English muffin, split
- 1/4 cup shredded Swiss cheese
- 1/4 cup sour cream
- 2 tablespoons mayonnaise
- 1 teaspoon lemon juice
- 2 slices deli ham (1 ounce *each*)
- 2 hard-cooked eggs, sliced

Paprika, optional

Place English muffin halves on a baking sheet. Sprinkle with cheese. Bake at 350° for 3-4 minutes or until cheese is melted.

Meanwhile, in a small bowl, combine the sour cream, mayonnaise and lemon juice. Place the ham and hard-cooked eggs on each muffin half; top with sour cream mixture. Sprinkle with paprika if desired. Bake for 15 minutes longer or until the muffins are heated through. **yield: 2 servings.**

ham 'n' egg muffins

blueberry cheesecake flapjacks

blueberry cheesecake flapjacks

Donna Cline • Pensacola, Florida
These flapjacks are so pretty, it's tempting to just gaze at them. But as good as they are to look at, they're even better to eat!

- 1 package (3 ounces) cream cheese, softened
- 3/4 cup whipped topping
- 1 cup all-purpose flour
- 1/2 cup graham cracker crumbs
- 1 tablespoon sugar
- 1 teaspoon baking powder
- 1/2 teaspoon baking soda
- 1/4 teaspoon salt
- 2 eggs, lightly beaten
- 1-1/4 cups buttermilk
- 1/4 cup butter, melted
- 1 cup fresh *or* frozen blueberries
- 3/4 cup maple syrup, warmed

Additional blueberries, optional

For topping, in a small bowl, beat cream cheese and whipped topping until smooth. Chill until serving.

In a large bowl, combine the flour, cracker crumbs, sugar, baking powder, baking soda and salt. Combine the eggs, buttermilk and butter; add to dry ingredients just until moistened. Fold in blueberries.

Pour batter by 1/4 cupfuls onto a greased hot griddle; turn when bubbles form on top. Cook until the second side is golden brown. Spread the topping over the pancakes. Top pancakes with warm syrup; sprinkle with additional blueberries if desired. **yield: 12 pancakes (3/4 cup topping).**

Editor's Note: If using frozen blueberries, do not thaw them before adding to the pancake batter. Be sure to thaw any berries used in the optional garnish.

hearty breakfast combo

Casey Ace • Rock Hill, New York

This dish is perfect for anyone who wants a taste of all the classic morning fare. My fiance's favorite meal is breakfast, so I created this recipe just for him.

    1   bacon strip, cut into 1-inch pieces
    1   sausage link, sliced
    1   small potato, halved lengthwise and thinly
        sliced
  1/4   cup chopped green pepper
    2   tablespoons chopped onion
  1/4   cup sliced fresh mushrooms
    1   slice cheddar cheese
    1   egg
Pepper to taste, optional

In a small nonstick skillet, cook the bacon and sausage over medium heat until the sausage is no longer pink. Add the potato, green pepper and onion; cook over medium-high heat for 10 minutes or until potato is browned. Stir in mushrooms; cook 1 minute longer. Top with cheddar cheese; cover and cook until the cheese is melted. Transfer to a plate; keep warm.

In the same skillet, add egg. Cook over medium heat just until egg white is set. Turn; cook 1-2 minutes longer or until completely set. Place egg on potato mixture; sprinkle with pepper if desired. **yield: 1 serving.**

hearty breakfast combo

maple cream coffee

maple cream coffee

Taste of Home Test Kitchen

On a crisp day, this creamy drink is the ideal way to warm up. Even non-coffee drinkers will enjoy the hint of maple and light coffee flavor in our home economists' top-pick beverage.

    3/4   cup half-and-half cream
    1/4   cup maple syrup
  1-1/4   cups brewed coffee
    1/4   cup whipped cream

In a small saucepan, cook and stir cream and syrup over medium heat until heated through. (Do not boil.) Divide evenly between two cups. Stir in coffee. Top with whipped cream. **yield: 2 servings.**

cottage cheese waffles

Lisabeth Hess • Chambersburg, Pennsylvania

Cottage cheese and extra eggs make these waffles soft and moist, with a slightly different texture than the usual variety. This is my family's preferred weekend treat, hands down.

    1   cup (8 ounces) cream-style cottage cheese,
        undrained
    6   eggs
  1/4   cup canola oil
  1/2   teaspoon vanilla extract
  1/2   cup all-purpose flour
  1/4   teaspoon salt
Maple syrup

In a blender, combine the cottage cheese, eggs, oil and vanilla. Cover and process until well combined. Add flour and salt; process until smooth.

Bake in a preheated waffle iron according to manufacturer's directions until golden brown. Serve with syrup. **yield: 4 waffles.**

Deanna Naivar
Temple, Texas
Suitable for any meal of the day, but especially welcomed at brunch, these crepes feature a rich chicken and broccoli filling everyone raves about.

chicken broccoli crepes

1 cup plus 2 tablespoons milk
2 eggs
2 tablespoons butter, melted
1 cup all-purpose flour
1/4 teaspoon salt
FILLING:
1/4 cup butter
1/4 cup all-purpose flour
2 cups chicken broth
2 teaspoons Worcestershire sauce
3 cups (12 ounces) shredded cheddar cheese, *divided*
2 cups (16 ounces) sour cream
2 packages (8 ounces *each*) frozen broccoli spears, cooked and drained
2-1/2 cups cubed cooked chicken

In a small bowl, beat milk, eggs and butter. Combine flour and salt; add to egg mixture and beat until smooth. Cover; refrigerate for 1 hour.

Heat a lightly greased 8-in. nonstick skillet. Stir batter; pour 1/4 cup into the center of skillet. Lift and tilt pan to evenly coat bottom. Cook until top appears dry; turn and cook 15-20 seconds longer. Remove to a wire rack. Repeat with remaining batter, greasing skillet as needed. When cool, stack crepes with waxed paper or paper towels in between.

In a large saucepan, melt butter. Stir in flour until smooth. Gradually stir in broth and Worcestershire sauce. Bring to a boil; cook and stir for 2 minutes or until thickened. Reduce heat; stir in 2 cups of cheese. Cook and stir for 10 minutes or until cheese is melted. Remove from the heat; stir in sour cream until smooth.

Place four broccoli spears and 1/3 cup of chicken down the center of each crepe; top with 1/3 cup cheese sauce. Roll up and place seam side down in a greased 13-in. x 9-in. baking dish. Pour remaining cheese sauce over crepes; sprinkle with remaining cheese. Bake, uncovered, at 350° for 20 minutes or until crepes are heated through. **yield: 8 crepes.**

omelet croissants

Edna Coburn • Tucson, Arizona

Crispy bacon and farm-fresh eggs never tasted so good as when they're stacked with cheese, greens, tomato and more in this grilled meal-in-one.

3	eggs
1	tablespoon water
1	teaspoon chicken bouillon granules
1	green onion, finely chopped
2	tablespoons finely chopped sweet red pepper
1/4	teaspoon lemon-pepper seasoning
1/2	teaspoon butter
2	croissants, split
4-1/2	teaspoons ranch salad dressing
4	slices Canadian bacon
4	slices Muenster cheese
1/2	cup fresh arugula
4	thin slices tomato

In a small bowl, whisk the eggs, water and bouillon; set aside. In a small nonstick skillet over medium heat, cook the green onion, red pepper and lemon-pepper seasoning in butter until tender.

Add egg mixture. As eggs set, push cooked edges toward the center, letting uncooked portion flow underneath. When eggs are completely set, fold omelet in half and cut into two wedges.

Spread croissants with salad dressing. On croissant bottoms, layer the bacon, omelet, cheese, arugula and tomato. Replace croissant tops.

Cook on a panini maker or indoor grill for 2-4 minutes or until cheese is melted. **yield: 2 servings.**

omelet croissants

roasted pepper, bacon & egg muffins

roasted pepper, bacon & egg muffins

Louise Gilbert • Quesnel, British Columbia

This healthy open-face sandwich is simple to prepare but packed with flavor. It's an easy way to start the day.

1/2	medium sweet red pepper
1/2	cup coarsely chopped sweet onion
1	teaspoon butter
4	egg whites
2	eggs
1	tablespoon fat-free milk
1/4	teaspoon pepper
2	center-cut bacon strips, cooked and crumbled
2	tablespoons shredded reduced-fat cheddar cheese
2	whole wheat English muffins, split and toasted

Remove and discard seeds from pepper half. Place cut side down on a baking sheet. Broil 4 in. from the heat until the skin blisters, about 6 minutes. Immediately place pepper half in a small bowl; cover and let stand for 15-20 minutes. Peel off and discard charred skin; chop pepper.

In a small nonstick skillet coated with cooking spray, saute onion in butter until tender. In a large bowl, whisk the egg whites, eggs, milk and pepper. Pour into the pan. Add bacon and chopped pepper; cook and stir over medium heat until eggs are completely set.

Remove from the heat. Sprinkle with cheese; cover and let stand until cheese is melted. Spoon onto English muffins. Serve immediately. **yield: 2 servings.**

multigrain pancakes

Jeri Tirmenstein • Apache Junction, Arizona
Oats and whole wheat flour make these tasty pancakes extra
hearty. Try them with applesauce in place of the traditional syrup.

- 1/4 **cup all-purpose flour**
- 1/4 **cup whole wheat flour**
- 1/4 **cup quick-cooking oats**
- 1 **tablespoon brown sugar**
- 1 **teaspoon baking powder**
- 1/4 **teaspoon salt**
- 1/2 **cup plus 1 tablespoon fat-free milk**
- 2 **tablespoons egg substitute**
- 2 **teaspoons canola oil**

In a large bowl, combine the first six ingredients. Combine the milk, egg substitute and oil; add to dry ingredients just until moistened.

Pour batter by 1/4 cupful onto a greased hot griddle. Turn when bubbles form on top; cook until the second side is golden brown. **yield: 4 pancakes.**

apple gorgonzola frittata

multigrain pancakes

apple gorgonzola frittata

Harry Renninger • La Plata, Maryland
After a few chilly days hiking in the Adirondack Mountains, I
got the idea for this recipe at a nearby diner, where they served
an apple omelet. I added my own touches, and this is the result.

- 4 **eggs, lightly beaten**
- 1/4 **cup heavy whipping cream**

Dash salt and pepper

- 1 **medium tart apple, peeled and finely chopped**
- 1/2 **teaspoon lemon juice**
- 1/3 **cup finely chopped onion**
- 1/3 **cup finely chopped celery**
- 1 **tablespoon olive oil**
- 1 **garlic clove, peeled**
- 1/3 **cup crumbled Gorgonzola cheese**

In a small bowl, whisk the eggs, cream, salt and pepper; set aside. In another bowl, toss apple with lemon juice; set aside.

In a 7-in. ovenproof skillet, saute the onion and celery in oil until tender. Add the garlic; cook 1 minute longer. Discard garlic.

Reduce heat. Add egg mixture to skillet; sprinkle with apple and cheese. Cover and cook for 4-6 minutes or until eggs are nearly set.

Uncover; broil 3-4 in. from the heat for 2-3 minutes or until eggs are completely set. Let stand for 5 minutes before cutting. **yield: 2 servings.**

dad's quick bagel omelet sandwich

Andrew Nodolski • Williamstown, New Jersey
I wrap these tasty sandwiches in aluminum foil and hand them out as the kids run for the school bus!

- 1/4 **cup finely chopped onion**
- 1 **tablespoon butter**
- 4 **eggs**
- 1/4 **cup chopped tomato**
- 1/8 **teaspoon salt**
- 1/8 **teaspoon hot pepper sauce**
- 4 **slices process American cheese**
- 4 **slices Canadian bacon**
- 4 **plain bagels, split**

In a large skillet, saute onion in butter until tender. Whisk the eggs, tomato, salt and hot pepper sauce. Add the egg mixture to the skillet (mixture should set immediately at edges).

As eggs set, push cooked edges toward the center, letting uncooked portion flow underneath. When the eggs are set, top with American cheese. Reduce heat; cover and cook for 1-2 minutes or until the cheese is melted. Meanwhile, heat bacon in the microwave and toast bagels if desired.

Cut the omelet into fourths and serve on split bagels with bacon. **yield: 4 servings.**

dad's quick bagel omelet sandwich

pumpkin waffles with orange walnut butter

pumpkin waffles with orange walnut butter

Brandi Davis • Pullman, Washington
Create smiles around the breakfast table with these unique and flavorful waffles. They're just right for autumn mornings.

- 1 **cup plus 2 tablespoons all-purpose flour**
- 2 **tablespoons brown sugar**
- 1 **teaspoon ground cinnamon**
- 1/2 **teaspoon salt**
- 1/2 **teaspoon baking powder**
- 1/4 **teaspoon baking soda**
- 2 **eggs**
- 1 **cup milk**
- 1/2 **cup canned pumpkin**
- 2 **tablespoons butter, melted**

ORANGE WALNUT BUTTER:
- 1/2 **cup butter, softened**
- 1/4 **cup chopped walnuts**
- 1 **tablespoon grated orange peel**

Maple syrup

In a large bowl, combine the first six ingredients. In another bowl, combine the eggs, milk, pumpkin and butter; stir into dry ingredients just until combined.

Bake in a preheated waffle iron according to manufacturer's directions until golden brown.

Meanwhile, for orange walnut butter, in a small bowl, combine the butter, walnuts and orange peel until blended. Serve waffles with butter mixture and maple syrup. **yield: 4 servings.**

biscuits with turkey sausage gravy

biscuits with turkey sausage gravy

Marcia Snyder • Boonton, New Jersey
When my husband was diagnosed with diabetes, I began using turkey sausage in this recipe. I tried it in this classic dish—needless to say, there are never any leftovers!

1	tube (16.3 ounces) large refrigerated flaky biscuits
1	pound Italian turkey sausage links, casings removed
3	tablespoons butter
3	tablespoons all-purpose flour
1/2	teaspoon ground mustard
1/4	teaspoon salt
1/8	teaspoon pepper
2-1/2	cups whole milk
1	tablespoon Worcestershire sauce

Bake biscuits according to package directions. Meanwhile, crumble sausage into a large saucepan; cook over medium heat until no longer pink. Drain and keep warm.

In the same saucepan, melt butter. Stir in the flour, mustard, salt and pepper until smooth. Gradually add milk and Worcestershire sauce. Bring to a boil; cook and stir for 2 minutes or until thickened.

Stir in sausage; heat through. Place two biscuits on each serving plate; top with gravy. **yield: 4 servings.**

pbj-stuffed french toast

Ruth Ann Bott • Lake Wales, Florida
I used some of my favorite foods to create this…and now it's become a favorite recipe to serve drop-in friends. They love it!

3	tablespoons cream cheese, softened
2	tablespoons creamy peanut butter
4	slices Italian bread (3/4 inch thick)
2	tablespoons red raspberry preserves
2	eggs, lightly beaten
1	tablespoon evaporated milk

Maple pancake syrup, optional

In a small bowl, combine cream cheese and peanut butter. Spread the mixture on two slices of bread; top with preserves and remaining bread. In a shallow bowl, whisk eggs and milk. Dip both sides of sandwiches into the egg mixture.

In a greased large nonstick skillet, toast sandwiches for 2-3 minutes on each side or until golden brown. Serve with syrup if desired. **yield: 2 servings.**

pbj-stuffed french toast

oh-so-good oatmeal

Danielle Pepa • Elgin, Illinois
Add extra nutrition to fiber-rich oatmeal by tossing in chopped apple and almonds. At 1-1/2 cups per serving, it's hearty and filling, has zero cholesterol—what's not to love? Your family will demand seconds.

- 3 **cups water**
- 2 **medium tart apples, chopped**
- 1-1/2 **cups old-fashioned oats**

Dash salt

- 1/4 **cup packed brown sugar**
- 1/2 **teaspoon ground cinnamon**
- 1/2 **teaspoon vanilla extract**
- 1/4 **cup chopped almonds**

Maple syrup *and/or* fat-free milk, optional

In a large saucepan over medium heat, bring the water to a boil. Add the chopped apples, oats and salt; cook and stir for 5 minutes.

Remove from the heat; stir in the brown sugar, cinnamon and vanilla. Cover and let oatmeal stand for 2 minutes. Sprinkle each serving with almonds. Serve with maple syrup and/or milk if desired. **yield: 4 servings.**

apple-bacon egg bake

Nancy Miller • Bettendorf, Iowa
I wanted an inexpensive, healthy egg dish for Sunday brunch, so I came with this recipe. The apples give it a slight sweetness, and the individual ramekins look so inviting.

- 3 **eggs**
- 1 **small apple, diced**
- 3/4 **cup frozen O'Brien potatoes, thawed**
- 1/3 **cup 2% milk**
- 1/3 **cup sour cream**
- 1/3 **cup shredded cheddar cheese, *divided***
- 3 **bacon strips, cooked and crumbled, *divided***

Dash salt and pepper

In a small bowl, beat the eggs. Stir in the apple, hash browns, milk, sour cream, 3 tablespoons cheese, 1 tablespoon bacon, salt and pepper.

Pour the egg mixture into two 2-cup baking dishes coated with cooking spray. Sprinkle with remaining cheddar cheese and bacon. Bake, uncovered, at 350° for 30-35 minutes or until a knife inserted near the center comes out clean. **yield: 2 servings.**

banana smoothie

banana smoothie

Ro Ann Cox • Lenoir, North Carolina

This has to be one of my best recipes because it can be made in a flash, yet it's incredibly delicious. The honey adds just the right amount of sweetness to the full banana flavor.

- 2 **cups milk**
- 2 **medium ripe bananas**
- 1/4 **cup honey**
- 1/2 **teaspoon vanilla extract**

Combine all ingredients in a blender until smooth. Stir if necessary. Pour into chilled glasses; serve immediately. **yield: 3-4 servings (3-1/2 cups).**

honey coffee

Taste of Home Test Kitchen

For a quick pick-me-up, sip this pleasantly sweet coffee, inspired by the taste of a traditional Spanish latte.

- 2 **cups hot strong brewed coffee (French or other dark roast)**
- 1/2 **cup milk**
- 1/4 **cup honey**
- 1/8 **teaspoon ground cinnamon**

Dash ground nutmeg

- 1/4 **teaspoon vanilla extract**

In a small saucepan, combine the coffee, milk, honey, cinnamon and nutmeg. Cook and stir until heated through. (Do not boil.) Remove from the heat; stir in vanilla. Pour into cups or mugs; serve immediately. **yield: 4 servings.**

puffy oven pancakes

Lillian Julow • Gainesville, Florida

Fluffy and pretty, with a refreshing hint of lemon, this berry-topped pancake is a cherished favorite for special occasions. What a wonderful way to start the morning!

- 2 **tablespoons butter**
- 2 **eggs**
- 1/2 **cup 2% milk**
- 1 **teaspoon grated lemon peel**
- 1/2 **teaspoon vanilla extract**
- 1/2 **cup all-purpose flour**
- 1/4 **cup fresh blueberries**
- 1/4 **cup fresh raspberries**
- 1/4 **cup sliced fresh strawberries**
- 1 **teaspoon confectioners' sugar**

Divide butter between two 2-cup round baking dishes. Place on a baking sheet. Heat in a 400° oven until the butter is melted.

In a small bowl, whisk the eggs, milk, lemon peel and vanilla. Whisk in flour until blended. Pour over butter. Bake, uncovered, for 14-16 minutes or until golden brown and puffy.

In a small bowl, gently combine the berries. Spoon onto pancakes; sprinkle with confectioners' sugar. **yield: 2 servings.**

puffy oven pancakes

Jenny Flake
Newport Beach,
California
This recipe is a family tradition, and has been for years. Besides being savory and hearty, these burritos are quick and easy to prepare!

brunch egg burritos

2 cups refrigerated shredded hash brown potatoes
3 tablespoons butter, *divided*
6 eggs
1/2 cup milk
1 can (4 ounces) chopped green chilies
1/4 teaspoon salt
1/4 teaspoon salt-free garlic seasoning blend
1/4 teaspoon pepper
4 to 6 drops Louisiana-style hot sauce
12 slices ready-to-serve fully cooked bacon, crumbled

2 cups (8 ounces) shredded Monterey Jack cheese
1 cup salsa
4 flour tortillas (10 inches), warmed

In a large skillet, cook potatoes in 2 tablespoons butter over medium heat for 6-7 minutes or until golden brown, stirring occasionally.

Meanwhile, in a small bowl, whisk the eggs, milk, chilies, seasonings and hot sauce. In another large skillet, heat remaining butter until hot. Add egg mixture; cook and stir over medium heat until eggs are completely set.

Layer 1/3 cup potatoes, about 1/2 cup egg mixture, 1/4 cup bacon, 1/2 cup cheese and 1/4 cup salsa off center on each tortilla. Fold sides and ends over filling and roll up. Serve immediately. **yield: 4 servings.**

butter pecan french toast

Cathy Hall • Phoenix, Arizona

Flavored coffee creamer is the secret ingredient in this fast-and-easy indulgence the whole family will enjoy. I sometimes substitute French-vanilla or caramel creamer, and add a little nutmeg and cinnamon to the eggs.

- 1 teaspoon plus 1 tablespoon butter, *divided*
- 1/2 cup chopped pecans
- 2 eggs
- 1/2 cup refrigerated Southern butter pecan nondairy creamer
- 6 slices French bread (1 inch thick)
- 1/4 cup confectioners' sugar
- 1/4 teaspoon ground cinnamon

Maple syrup, optional

In a small skillet, melt 1 teaspoon butter over medium heat. Add the chopped pecans; cook and stir for 3 minutes or until toasted.

In a shallow bowl, whisk eggs and creamer. Dip both sides of each slice of bread in egg mixture. In a large skillet, melt remaining butter over medium heat. Cook bread for 2-3 minutes on each side or until golden brown. Sprinkle with toasted pecans, confectioners' sugar and ground cinnamon. Serve with maple syrup if desired. **yield: 3 servings.**

butter pecan french toast

hash brown breakfast casserole

hash brown breakfast casserole

Cindy Schneider • Sarasota, Florida

This savory, scrumptious breakfast bake uses egg substitute for lower fat and cholesterol. Serve slices with fresh fruit for a meal that will keep your gang satisfied until lunch!

- 4 cups frozen shredded hash brown potatoes, thawed
- 1-1/2 cups egg substitute
- 1 cup finely chopped cooked chicken breast
- 1/2 teaspoon garlic powder
- 1/2 teaspoon pepper
- 3/4 cup shredded reduced-fat cheddar cheese

In a large bowl, combine hash browns, egg substitute, chicken, garlic powder and pepper. Transfer mixture to an 8-in. square baking dish coated with cooking spray; sprinkle with cheese.

Bake, uncovered, at 350° for 40-45 minutes or a knife inserted near the center comes out clean. Let stand for 5 minutes before serving. **yield: 4 servings.**

bistro breakfast panini

Kathy Harding • Richmond, Missouri

I tried an omelet that contained Brie, bacon and apples and thought it would be tasty as a breakfast panini—I was right! Now it's a frequent morning treat.

6	bacon strips
1	teaspoon butter
4	eggs, lightly beaten
4	slices sourdough bread (3/4 inch thick)
1/8	teaspoon salt
1/8	teaspoon pepper
3	ounces Brie cheese, thinly sliced
8	thin slices apple
1/2	cup fresh baby spinach
2	tablespoons butter, softened

In a large skillet, cook bacon over medium heat until crisp. Remove to paper towels to drain.

Meanwhile, heat butter in a large skillet over medium heat. Add eggs; cook and stir until set.

Place eggs on two slices of bread; sprinkle with salt and pepper. Layer with cheese, apple, bacon, spinach and remaining bread. Butter outsides of sandwiches.

Cook on a panini maker or indoor grill for 3-4 minutes or until the bread is browned and the cheese is melted. **yield: 2 servings.**

bistro breakfast panini

ham 'n' cheese crepes

ham 'n' cheese crepes

Marion Lowery • Medford, Oregon

These thin, delicate pancakes are easy to freeze and thaw, which makes it a breeze to cook up a batch, prepare just enough for two and save the rest of the crepes for another time.

1/3	cup cold water
1/3	cup plus 2 to 3 tablespoons 2% milk, *divided*
1/2	cup all-purpose flour
1	egg
2	tablespoons butter, melted
1/8	teaspoon salt

ADDITIONAL INGREDIENTS (for 4 crepes):

1	tablespoon Dijon mustard
4	thin slices deli ham
1/2	cup shredded cheddar cheese

In a blender, combine the water, 1/3 cup milk, flour, egg, butter and salt; cover and process until smooth. Refrigerate for at least 30 minutes; stir. Add remaining milk if batter is too thick.

Heat a lightly greased 8-in. skillet; add about 3 tablespoons batter. Lift and tilt pan to evenly coat bottom. Cook until top appears dry; turn and cook 15-20 seconds longer. Repeat with remaining batter, greasing skillet as needed. Stack four crepes with waxed paper in between; cover and freeze for up to 3 months.

Spread Dijon mustard over remaining crepes; top each with ham and cheese. Roll up tightly. Place crepes in an 8-in. square baking dish coated with cooking spray. Bake, uncovered, at 375° for 10-14 minutes.

To use frozen crepes: Thaw crepes in the refrigerator for about 2 hours. Fill crepes and bake as directed. **yield: 4 filled crepes plus 4 unfilled crepes.**

raspberry french toast cups

raspberry french toast cups

Sandi Tuttle • Hayward, Wisconsin

These singular sensations are a delightful twist on the usual recipe and definitely make any morning unique. When fresh raspberries are available, I like to sprinkle additional berries on top of the French toast.

> 2 slices Italian bread, cut into 1/2-inch cubes
> 1/2 cup fresh *or* frozen raspberries
> 2 ounces cream cheese, cut into 1/2-inch cubes
> 2 eggs
> 1/2 cup milk
> 1 tablespoon maple syrup
> **RASPBERRY SYRUP:**
> 2 teaspoons cornstarch
> 1/3 cup water
> 2 cups fresh *or* frozen raspberries, *divided*
> 1 tablespoon lemon juice
> 1 tablespoon maple syrup
> 1/2 teaspoon grated lemon peel
> **Ground cinnamon, optional**

Divide half of the bread cubes between two greased 8-oz. custard cups. Sprinkle with raspberries and cream cheese. Top with remaining bread. In a small bowl, whisk the eggs, milk and syrup; pour over bread. Cover and refrigerate for at least 1 hour.

Remove from the refrigerator 30 minutes before baking. Bake, uncovered, at 350° for 25-30 minutes or until golden brown.

Meanwhile, in a small saucepan, combine cornstarch and water until smooth. Add 1-1/2 cups raspberries,

lemon juice, syrup and lemon peel. Bring to a boil; reduce heat. Cook and stir for 2 minutes or until thickened. Strain and discard seeds; cool slightly.

Gently stir the remaining berries into syrup. Sprinkle French toast cups with cinnamon if desired; serve with syrup. **yield: 2 servings.**

eggs lorraine

Sandra Woolard • DeLand, Florida

This has to be one of my favorite special-occasion dishes. It's absolutely delicious, and the presentation is so pretty!

> 4 slices Canadian bacon
> 2 slices Swiss cheese
> 4 eggs
> 2 tablespoons sour cream
> 1/8 teaspoon salt
> 1/8 teaspoon pepper
> **Minced chives, optional**

Coat two shallow oval 1-1/2-cup baking dishes with cooking spray. Line with Canadian bacon; top with cheese. Carefully break two eggs into each dish.

In a small bowl, whisk sour cream, salt and pepper until smooth; drop by teaspoonfuls onto eggs.

Bake, uncovered, at 350° for 25-30 minutes or until eggs are completely set. Sprinkle with chives if desired. **yield: 2 servings.**

eggs lorraine

crabmeat scramble

crabmeat scramble

Macey Allen • Green Forest, Arkansas

We enjoy this elegant twist to ordinary scrambled eggs every Sunday. The rich-tasting speciality is no fuss to make and requires only simple ingredients.

    4   eggs
  1/4   cup sour cream
    2   tablespoons grated Parmesan cheese
  1/4   teaspoon pepper
  1/8   teaspoon salt
    1   can (6 ounces) lump crabmeat, drained
    2   tablespoons sliced green onion
    2   tablespoons butter

In a small bowl, whisk the eggs, sour cream, cheese, pepper and salt; set aside.

In a large skillet, saute crab and onion in butter until crab is lightly browned and onion is tender. Add egg mixture; cook and stir over medium heat until eggs are completely set. **yield: 2 servings.**

twice-baked cheese souffles

Taste of Home Test Kitchen

You'll easily impress guests with these individual cheese souffles from our home economists. Partially bake and refrigerate them early in the morning. Then simply sprinkle with cheese and finish baking when ready to eat.

    3   tablespoons butter
  1/4   cup all-purpose flour
    2   cups plus 2 tablespoons milk
  1/4   teaspoon onion powder
  1/4   teaspoon salt
  1/8   teaspoon ground nutmeg
  1/8   teaspoon pepper
    2   cups (8 ounces) shredded cheddar cheese, *divided*
    3   eggs, *separated*

In a large saucepan, melt butter. Stir in the flour until smooth. Gradually add milk, onion powder, salt, nutmeg and pepper. Bring to a boil; cook and stir for 2 minutes or until thickened. Reduce heat; add 1 cup shredded cheddar cheese and stir until melted. Remove from the heat; set aside.

In a small bowl, beat egg yolks until thick and lemon-colored, about 3 minutes. Stir in 1/3 cup hot cheese sauce. Return all to the pan; cook and stir for 1-2 minutes. Cool completely.

In large bowl, beat egg whites on high speed until stiff peaks form. Gently fold into cooled cheese mixture. Pour into ungreased 1-cup souffle dishes or custard cups. Place in a shallow baking pan. Add 1 in. of hot water to pan.

Bake, uncovered, at 325° for 20 minutes. Remove custard cups to wire racks to cool. Cover and refrigerate for up to 4 hours.

Remove from the refrigerator 30 minutes before baking. Uncover; sprinkle with remaining cheese. Bake at 425° for 15-20 minutes or until puffed and golden brown. **yield: 4 servings.**

twice-baked cheese souffles

appetizers & snacks

Rely on the pared-down yet delicious recipes featured here to give all your small gatherings and special meals a memorable beginning.

gouda melt with baguette slices, page 25

refreshing tomato bruschetta

cooking tip

When a recipe calls for a clove of garlic and you don't have any fresh bulbs, substitute 1/4 teaspoon of garlic powder for each clove. Next time you're shopping, look for convenient jars of fresh minced galic in the produce section. Use 1/2 teaspoon of minced garlic for each clove.

Greta Igl
Menomonee Falls,
Wisconsin
People agree this recipe is best with sun-warmed tomatoes and basil fresh from the garden. My husband and I love this so much, we can make a meal of it alone!

refreshing tomato bruschetta

3 teaspoons olive oil, *divided*
4 slices French bread (1/2 inch thick)
1 garlic clove, cut in half lengthwise
3/4 cup chopped seeded tomato
1 tablespoon minced fresh basil
1/2 teaspoon minced fresh parsley
1/2 teaspoon red wine vinegar
1/8 teaspoon salt
1/8 teaspoon pepper

Brush 2 teaspoons oil over one side of each slice of bread; place bread on a baking sheet. Bake at 350° for 5-7 minutes or until lightly browned. Rub cut side of garlic over bread.

Meanwhile, in a small bowl, combine the tomato, basil, parsley, vinegar, salt, pepper and remaining oil. Spoon onto bread; serve immediately. **yield: 2 servings.**

fruit kabobs with margarita dip

Michelle Zapf • Kingsland, Georgia
Your adult guests will love the margarita flavor of this cool and creamy dip. We even serve the kabobs as dessert.

- 1   package (3 ounces) cream cheese, softened
- 1/2 cup sour cream
- 1/4 cup confectioners' sugar
- 1   tablespoon lime juice
- 1   tablespoon thawed orange juice concentrate
- 1   tablespoon tequila
- 1/2 cup heavy whipping cream
- 12 fresh strawberries
- 6   pineapple chunks
- 1   medium mango, peeled and cubed
- 6   seedless red grapes
- 2   slices pound cake, cubed

In a large bowl, combine the first six ingredients. Beat in whipping cream until fluffy. Alternately, thread fruits and cake on metal or wooden skewers. Serve with dip. **yield: 6 kabobs (1-1/2 cups dip).**

fruit kabobs with margarita dip

crab-stuffed cherry tomatoes

crab-stuffed cherry tomatoes

Marcia Keckhaver • Burlington, Wisconsin
For a little something special, I include these petite pleasers on the menu of all of our parties.

- 1   pint cherry tomatoes
- 1   can (6 ounces) crabmeat, drained, flaked and cartilage removed
- 1/2 cup diced green pepper
- 2   green onions, diced
- 2   tablespoons seasoned bread crumbs
- 1   teaspoon white wine vinegar
- 1/2 teaspoon dried parsley flakes
- 1/4 teaspoon dill weed
- 1/8 teaspoon salt, optional

Cut a thin slice off the top of each cherry tomato. Scoop out the pulp, leaving a 1/2-in. shell. Invert tomatoes onto paper towels to drain. In a small bowl, combine the remaining ingredients.

Stuff the tomatoes with crabmeat mixture; place in an ungreased 13-in. x 9-in. baking dish. Bake, uncovered, at 350° for 8-10 minutes or until heated through. Serve warm. **yield: about 1-1/2 dozen.**

toasted ravioli

Kathy Morgan • Oceanside, California

This recipe originally called for 13 ingredients, but I found a much faster way to make these tasty treats. Since they're toasted in the oven instead of a deep fryer, they're healthier, too.

- 8 frozen cheese ravioli
- 2 tablespoons Italian salad dressing
- 1 tablespoon seasoned bread crumbs
- 1/2 cup marinara sauce, warmed

Cook ravioli according to package directions; drain. Place ravioli on a baking sheet coated with cooking spray. Brush tops with Italian salad dressing; sprinkle with bread crumbs.

Bake at 350° for 12-15 minutes or until golden brown. Serve with marinara sauce. **yield: 2 servings.**

five-spice pecans

Anne Leslie • Chandler, Indiana

Talk about a sugar-and-spice indulgence! Just try to stop eating these toasty, munchable nuts. They are also great sprinkled on different kinds of salads.

- 2 cups pecan halves
- 2 tablespoons brown sugar
- 2 tablespoons maple syrup
- 1 teaspoon Chinese five-spice powder

In a large nonstick skillet, cook pecans over medium heat until toasted, about 4 minutes. Add the brown sugar, syrup and five-spice powder. Cook and stir nuts for 2-4 minutes or until sugar is melted. Spread on foil to cool. Store in an airtight container. **yield: 2 cups.**

five-spice pecans

baked deli sandwich

baked deli sandwich

Sandra McKenzie • Braham, Minnesota

Frozen bread dough, easy assembly and a quick baking time make this stuffed sandwich an appetizer I rely on often. This is one of my most-requested recipes. It's easy to double for a crowd or to experiment with different meats and cheeses.

- 1 loaf (1 pound) frozen bread dough, thawed
- 2 tablespoons butter, melted
- 1/4 teaspoon garlic salt
- 1/4 teaspoon dried basil
- 1/4 teaspoon dried oregano
- 1/4 teaspoon pizza seasoning *or* Italian seasoning
- 1/4 pound sliced deli ham
- 6 thin slices part-skim mozzarella cheese
- 1/4 pound sliced deli smoked turkey breast
- 6 thin slices cheddar cheese

Pizza sauce, warmed, optional

On a baking sheet coated with cooking spray, roll dough into a small rectangle. Let rest for 5-10 minutes.

In a small bowl, combine the butter and seasonings. Roll out dough into a 14-in. x 10-in. rectangle. Brush with half of the butter mixture. Layer ham, mozzarella cheese, turkey and cheddar cheese lengthwise over half of the dough to within 1/2 in. of edges. Fold dough over and pinch firmly to seal. Brush with remaining butter mixture.

Bake at 400° for 10-12 minutes or until golden brown. Cut into 1-in. slices. Serve immediately with pizza sauce if desired. **yield: 4-6 servings.**

roasted goat cheese with garlic

Mash garlic mixture with a fork. Stir in the vinegar, salt and pepper. Transfer to a serving bowl; sprinkle with basil. Serve warm with French bread or assorted crackers. **yield: about 1-1/4 cups.**

pepperoni roll-ups

Debra Purcell • Safford, Arizona
Here is a fast hors d'oeuvre recipe that goes over well at my house. Each bite has gooey, melted cheese and real pizza flavor. Try serving the tasty bites with pizza sauce for dipping.

- 1 tube (8 ounces) refrigerated crescent rolls
- 16 slices pepperoni, cut into quarters
- 2 pieces string cheese (1 ounce *each*), cut into quarters
- 3/4 teaspoon Italian seasoning, *divided*
- 1/4 teaspoon garlic salt

Unroll crescent dough; separate into eight triangles. Place eight pepperoni pieces on each. Place a piece of cheese on the long side of each triangle; sprinkle with 1/2 teaspoon Italian seasoning. Roll up each, starting with a long side; pinch seams to seal. Sprinkle with garlic salt and remaining Italian seasoning.

Place 2 in. apart on a greased baking sheet. Bake at 375° for 10-12 minutes or until golden brown. Serve warm. **yield: 8 appetizers.**

lemony hummus

Josephine Piro • Easton, Pennsylvania
This easy hummus is flavored with garlic and lemon, and it has a delicious nuttiness from tahini. I love the flavor's subtle kick!

- 2 garlic cloves, peeled
- 1 can (15 ounces) chickpeas *or* garbanzo beans, rinsed and drained
- 1/4 cup lemon juice
- 3 tablespoons water
- 2 tablespoons tahini
- 1 teaspoon ground cumin
- 1/4 teaspoon salt
- 1/4 teaspoon pepper
- **Pita breads, warmed and cut into wedges**
- **Carrot and celery sticks**

Process garlic in a food processor until minced. Add the chickpeas, lemon juice, water, tahini, cumin, salt and pepper; cover and process until smooth. Transfer to a small bowl. Serve with pita wedges and vegetables. **yield: 1-1/2 cups.**

roasted goat cheese with garlic

Carol Barlow • Berwyn, Illinois
Now that we have kids, my husband and I don't entertain much. But when we do, I serve this savory spread. The combination of goat cheese, garlic and onions always earns rave reviews from our guests.

- 6 to 8 garlic cloves, peeled
- 1 tablespoon canola oil
- 1 medium red onion, thinly sliced
- 2 tablespoons butter
- 1 tablespoon brown sugar
- 8 ounces crumbled goat *or* feta cheese
- 1 tablespoon white balsamic vinegar
- **Salt and pepper to taste**
- 1/4 cup thinly sliced fresh basil
- **Thinly sliced French bread *or* assorted crackers**

Place garlic and oil in a pie plate. Cover and bake at 350° for 30 minutes.

Meanwhile, in a small skillet, saute onion in butter until tender and lightly browned. Add brown sugar; cook and stir until sugar is dissolved. Remove from the heat.

Remove garlic from pie plate. Spread onion mixture in pie plate; top with goat or feta cheese. Place garlic over cheese. Bake, uncovered, for 15-20 minutes or until cheese is melted.

chive crab cakes

chive crab cakes

Cindy Worth • Lapwai, Idaho
These tasty crab cakes are perfect for appetizers, or try them with a salad for a light meal. They're fantastic either way.

- 4 egg whites
- 1 egg
- 6 tablespoons minced chives
- 3 tablespoons all-purpose flour
- 1 to 2 teaspoons hot pepper sauce
- 1 teaspoon baking powder
- 1/2 teaspoon salt
- 1/4 teaspoon pepper
- 4 cans (6 ounces *each*) crabmeat, drained, flaked and cartilage removed
- 2 cups panko (Japanese) bread crumbs
- 2 tablespoons canola oil

In a large bowl, lightly beat the egg whites and egg. Add the chives, flour, pepper sauce, baking powder, salt and pepper; mix well. Fold in crab. Cover and refrigerate for at least 2 hours.

Place bread crumbs in a shallow bowl. Drop crab mixture by 1/4 cupfuls into crumbs. Gently coat and shape into 3/4-in.-thick patties.

In a large nonstick skillet, cook crab cakes in oil in batches over medium-high heat for 3-4 minutes on each side or until golden brown. **yield: 6 servings.**

black bean-mango salad

Donna Hollon • Port Orchard, Washington
This fresh-tasting salad is a lively side dish for chicken or fish. Simple to put together and pack for a picnic, it's a yummy way to slip more fruit and veggies into meals.

- 2 medium mangoes, peeled and cubed
- 1 cup canned black beans, rinsed and drained

- 1/4 cup finely chopped sweet red pepper
- 2 tablespoons finely chopped red onion
- 2 tablespoons minced fresh cilantro
- 2 tablespoons orange juice
- 1 tablespoon finely chopped jalapeno pepper
- 1 tablespoon lime juice
- 1/8 teaspoon ground cumin

Dash salt

In a small bowl, combine all ingredients. Refrigerate until serving. **yield: 4 servings.**

Editor's Note: When cutting hot peppers, disposable gloves are recommended. Avoid touching your face.

gouda melt with baguette slices

Susan Lewis • Reading, Pennsylvania
This fun starter is guaranteed to wow friends! It takes just moments to whip up this melty delight.

- 1 French bread baguette (4 ounces), sliced
- 1 round (7 ounces) Gouda cheese
- 1 plum tomato, seeded and chopped
- 1 tablespoon minced fresh basil

Place baguette slices on an ungreased baking sheet. Broil 3-4 in. from the heat for 1-2 minutes on each side or until toasted.

Meanwhile, carefully remove waxed coating from cheese round. Using a 3-in. biscuit cutter, press into the center of cheese, but not all the way through. Scoop out center, leaving a 1/4-in. shell; set shell aside.

Place the tomato, basil and removed cheese in a small microwave-safe bowl. Cover and microwave on high for 1 minute or until cheese is melted. Stir until combined; pour cheese mixture into shell. Serve with baguette toasts. **yield: 4 servings.**

gouda melt with baguette slices

grilled potato skins

cooking tip

2

To mince fresh herbs, such as rosemary for Grilled Potato Skins, hold the handle of a chef's knife with one hand, and rest the finger of your other hand on the top of the blade near the tip. Using the handle to guide and apply pressure, move the knife in an arc across the bunch of fresh herbs with a rocking motion until pieces are no larger than 1/8 in.

Mitzi Sentiff
Annapollis, Maryland
Everyone just loves this party food favorite. They're the ideal addition to any cookout's menu.

grilled potato skins

2 **large baking potatoes**
2 **tablespoons butter, melted**
2 **teaspoons minced fresh rosemary** *or* 1/2 **teaspoon dried rosemary, crushed**
1/2 **teaspoon salt**
1/2 **teaspoon pepper**
1 **cup (4 ounces) shredded cheddar cheese**
3 **bacon strips, cooked and crumbled**
2 **green onions, chopped**
Sour cream

Cut each potato lengthwise into four wedges. Cut away the white portion, leaving 1/4 in. on the potato skins. Place the potatoe skins on a microwave-safe plate. Microwave, uncovered, on high for 8-10 minutes or until tender. Combine the butter, rosemary, salt and pepper; brush over both sides of potato skins.

Grill the potatoes, skin side up, uncovered, over direct medium heat for 2-3 minutes or until lightly browned. Turn the potatoes and position them over indirect heat; grill 2 minutes longer. Top with cheddar cheese. Cover and grill 2-3 minutes longer or until cheese is melted. Sprinkle with bacon and onions. Serve potato skins with sour cream. **yield: 8 appetizers.**

Editor's Note: This recipe was tested in a 1,100-watt microwave.

bacon jalapeno poppers

Bernice Knutson • Danbury, Iowa
For a delicious starter for two, try these spicy bites. The bacon adds a smoky flavor to the traditional cheesy popper.

- 2 bacon strips, halved
- 2 jalapeno peppers, halved lengthwise and seeded
- 4 teaspoons shredded Colby cheese
- 4 teaspoons cream cheese, softened

In a small skillet, cook bacon over medium heat until partially cooked but not crisp. Remove to paper towels to drain; keep warm.

Combine cheeses; spread into each pepper half. Wrap a piece of bacon around each pepper half. Place on a baking sheet.

Bake, uncovered, at 350° for 20-25 minutes or until the bacon is crisp and the cheese filling is heated through. **yield: 2 servings.**

Editor's Note: When cutting hot peppers, disposable gloves are recommended. Avoid touching your face.

deep-fried onions with dipping sauce

Taste of Home Test Kitchen
Enjoy this common steakhouse appetizer right in your own home. Our home economists covered onion wedges with a golden batter and fried them to crispy perfection. The spicy dipping sauce really heats things up!

- 1 sweet onion
- 1/2 cup all-purpose flour
- 1 teaspoon paprika
- 1/2 teaspoon garlic powder
- 1/8 teaspoon cayenne pepper
- 1/8 teaspoon pepper

BEER BATTER:
- 1/3 cup all-purpose flour
- 1 tablespoon cornstarch
- 1/2 teaspoon garlic powder
- 1/2 teaspoon paprika
- 1/4 teaspoon salt
- 1/4 teaspoon pepper
- 7 tablespoons beer *or* nonalcoholic beer

Oil for frying

DIPPING SAUCE:
- 1/4 cup sour cream
- 2 tablespoons chili sauce
- 1/4 teaspoon ground cumin
- 1/8 teaspoon cayenne pepper

Cut onion into 1-in. wedges and separate into pieces. In a shallow bowl, combine the flour, paprika, garlic powder, cayenne and pepper.

For batter, in another shallow bowl, combine the flour, cornstarch, garlic powder, paprika, salt and pepper. Stir in beer. Dip onions into flour mixture, then into batter and again into flour mixture.

In an electric skillet or deep-fat fryer, heat oil to 375°. Fry onions, a few at a time, for 1-2 minutes on each side or until golden brown. Drain on paper towels. In a bowl, combine sauce ingredients. Serve with onions. **yield: 2 servings.**

deep-fried onions with dipping sauce

mango salsa

Microwave on high for 3 minutes; turn and microwave 2-3 minutes longer or until chips are dry and brittle. Repeat with remaining potatoes, oil and seasonings. Let chips cool for at least 1 minute before serving. Store in an airtight container. **yield: 5 servings.**

Cumin Crunch Potato Chips: Substitute garlic powder and ground cumin for the curry powder.

Nice & Spiced Potato Chips: Substitute chili powder and ground chipotle pepper for the curry powder.

Editor's Note: This recipe was tested in a 1,100-watt microwave.

mango salsa

Kristine Sims • St. Joseph, Michigan
I put a tantalizing twist on salsa with this recipe. Tangy fruit, savory onion and peppy hot sauce work in perfect harmony to create a fun appetizer that's good for you, too!

- 1/2 cup finely chopped tart apple
- 1/2 cup finely chopped peeled mango
- 1/2 cup canned crushed pineapple
- 2 green onions, thinly sliced
- 2 tablespoons minced fresh cilantro
- 3 to 5 drops hot pepper sauce, optional

Tortilla chips

In a small bowl, combine the apple, mango, pineapple, onions, cilantro and pepper sauce if desired. Chill until serving. Serve with tortilla chips. **yield: 1-1/2 cups.**

microwave potato chips

Taste of Home Test Kitchen
Can you make golden, crunchy homemade potato chips in the microwave? We had our doubts, but they were quickly put to rest by this simple recipe whipped up by our home economists!

- 3 medium red potatoes
- 1/4 cup olive oil
- 1 teaspoon salt

Curry powder

Layer three paper towels on a microwave-safe plate; set the plate aside.

Scrub potatoes and cut into 1/16-in.-thick slices. Brush slices on both sides with olive oil and lightly sprinkle with salt and curry. Arrange the potatoes on prepared plate (do not overlap).

cinnamon baked pretzels

Marina Heppner • Orchard Park, New York
This delicious recipe is almost as fun to make as it is to eat! It's a great brunch starter or perfect for the morning after the kids have a slumber party.

- 3 tablespoons cinnamon-sugar
- 2 tablespoons butter
- 1/4 teaspoon ground nutmeg
- 1 package (13 ounces) frozen baked soft pretzels
- 1/2 cup red raspberry preserves, warmed

In a small microwave-safe bowl, combine the cinnamon-sugar, butter and nutmeg. Microwave, uncovered, on high for 30-45 seconds or until butter is melted; brush over pretzels. Transfer to an ungreased baking sheet.

Bake at 400° for 3-4 minutes or until heated through. Serve with preserves. **yield: 6 pretzels.**

cinnamon baked pretzels

fried onion rings

Christine Wilson • Sellersville, Pennsylvania
Sweet Vidalia onion rings are deep-fried to a crispy golden brown, then served with a cool and zesty lime dipping sauce.

- 1 large Vidalia *or* sweet onion
- 3/4 cup all-purpose flour
- 1/4 cup cornmeal
- 1/2 teaspoon baking powder
- 1/2 teaspoon salt
- 1/4 teaspoon baking soda
- 1/4 teaspoon cayenne pepper
- 1 egg
- 1 cup buttermilk

Oil for frying

LIME DIPPING SAUCE:
- 2/3 cup mayonnaise
- 3 tablespoons honey
- 2 tablespoons lime juice
- 2 tablespoons spicy brown *or* horseradish mustard
- 1 teaspoon prepared horseradish

Cut onion into 1/2 in. slices; separate into rings. In a large bowl, combine the flour, cornmeal, baking powder, salt, baking soda and cayenne. Combine egg and buttermilk. Stir egg mixture into dry ingredients just until moistened.

In an electric skillet or deep-fat fryer, heat 1 in. of oil to 375°. Dip onion rings into batter. Fry a few at a time for 1 to 1-1/2 minutes on each side or until golden brown. Drain on paper towels (keep warm in a 300° oven).

In a small bowl, combine sauce ingredients. Serve with onion rings. Serve immediately. **yield: 4 servings.**

chunky bloody mary salsa

Jessie Apfel • Berkeley, California
Lemon and lime juices lend a citrus tang to this simple salsa, while horseradish gives it a little kick.

- 1 teaspoon prepared horseradish
- 1 teaspoon lemon juice
- 1/2 teaspoon lime juice
- 1/2 teaspoon Worcestershire sauce
- 2 to 3 drops hot pepper sauce
- 2 medium tomatoes, seeded and chopped
- 9 green onions, chopped
- 1/4 teaspoon salt

Tortilla chips

In a small bowl, combine the first five ingredients. Stir in the tomatoes, onions and salt. Refrigerate until serving.

Transfer to a serving bowl with a slotted spoon; serve with tortilla chips. **yield: 1-1/2 cups.**

almond cheese spread

Joan Cooper • Lake Orion, Michigan
I love this dip recipe! It's a great way to use up leftover or different kinds of cheeses I've already got on hand.

- 1/2 cup shredded sharp white cheddar cheese
- 2 tablespoons mayonnaise
- 1/8 teaspoon onion powder

Dash pepper

Dash Louisiana-style hot sauce
- 1 green onion, chopped
- 1 tablespoon sliced almonds

Celery ribs *or* assorted crackers

In a small bowl, combine the first five ingredients; stir in the green onion and sliced almonds. Cover; refrigerate for at least 4 hours. Serve cheese spread with celery or crackers. **yield: 2 servings.**

almond cheese spread

hot 'n' spicy cranberry dip

Marian Platt • Sequim, Washington

When I want to make this as an hors d'oeuvre for a special occasion or party, I double the recipe, using one 16-ounce can of cranberry sauce.

3/4	cup jellied cranberry sauce
1	to 2 tablespoons prepared horseradish
1	tablespoon honey
1-1/2	teaspoons lemon juice
1-1/2	teaspoons Worcestershire sauce
1/8	to 1/4 teaspoon cayenne pepper
1	garlic clove, minced

Miniature hot dogs *or* **smoked sausage links, warmed**
Sliced apples *or* **pears**

In a small saucepan, combine the first seven ingredients; bring to a boil, stirring constantly. Reduce heat. Cover; simmer for 5 minutes, stirring occasionally. Serve the dip warm with miniature sausages and/or sliced fruit. **yield: 3/4 cup.**

basil parmesan shrimp

Laura Hamilton • Belleville, Ontario

This recipe is a nice light way to serve shrimp. The fresh basil adds a sweet taste, while the vinegar gives it a nice tang.

1/2	cup olive oil, *divided*
1/4	cup minced fresh basil
1	tablespoon white vinegar
1	tablespoon plus 1/2 cup grated Parmesan cheese, *divided*
1/2	teaspoon sugar
1	pound uncooked large shrimp, peeled and deveined
1/4	cup butter, cubed

Lettuce leaves

Combine 1/4 cup oil, basil, vinegar, 1 tablespoon cheese and sugar in a saucepan over low heat. Meanwhile, combine shrimp and remaining cheese.

In a large skillet, heat butter and remaining oil. Add shrimp; saute for 3-4 minutes or until shrimp turn pink. Drain on paper towels. Serve on lettuce; drizzle with warm dressing. **yield: 4-6 servings.**

mushroom puffs

mushroom puffs

Marilin Rosborough • Altoona, Pennsylvania

You can make these attractive appetizers in just minutes with refrigerated crescent roll dough. The tasty little pinwheels disappear fast at parties.

4	ounces cream cheese, cubed
1	can (4 ounces) mushroom stems and pieces, drained
1	tablespoon chopped onion
1/8	teaspoon hot pepper sauce
1	tube (8 ounces) crescent roll dough

In a blender, combine the cream cheese, mushrooms, onion and hot pepper sauce; cover and process until blended. Unroll crescent dough; separate into four rectangles. Press perforations to seal. Spread mushroom mixture over dough.

Roll up jelly-roll style, starting with a long side. Cut each roll into five slices; place on an ungreased baking sheet. Bake at 425° for 8-10 minutes or until puffed and golden brown. **yield: 20 appetizers.**

corn salsa tostadas

cooking tip

If you have more fresh cilantro than you can use right away, freezing rather than drying it will retain more of its distinctive flavor. To freeze, wash and drain whole sprigs, then pat dry with paper towels. Place a few sprigs at a time into small plastic freezer bags and freeze. Or chop cilantro and freeze in ice cube trays. Place a tablespoon of the herb in each section, then cover with water and freeze.

Laurie Todd
Columbus, Mississippi
These south-of-the-border treats are sure to satisfy cravings for something a little spicy. The bite-size morsels are tasty, attractive and fun to eat.

corn salsa tostadas

3	flour tortillas (8 inches)
3/4	cup fat-free sour cream
3	teaspoons minced fresh cilantro, *divided*
2	green onions, finely chopped
1/4	teaspoon garlic powder
3/4	cup fresh *or* frozen corn, thawed
1	plum tomato, diced
1	tablespoon chopped jalapeno pepper
2	tablespoons orange juice
1	teaspoon canola oil
1/2	teaspoon salt

Using a 2-in. round cookie cutter, cut 12 circles from each tortilla. Coat both sides of circles with cooking spray. Place in a single layer on a baking sheet. Bake at 400° for 4-5 minutes or until crisp. Cool.

In a small bowl, combine the sour cream, 1 teaspoon cilantro, onions and garlic powder; cover and refrigerate. In another bowl, combine the corn, tomato, jalapeno, orange juice, oil, salt and remaining cilantro; cover and refrigerate. Just before serving, spread 1 teaspoon sour cream mixture over each tostada. Using a slotted spoon, top each with a teaspoonful of corn salsa. **yield: 3 dozen.**

Editor's Note: When cutting hot peppers, disposable gloves are recommended. Avoid touching your face.

coconut fried shrimp

bacon roll-ups

Janet Abate • North Brunswick, New Jersey
This family favorite dates back to the 1930s, when my grandmother started making these yummy morsels.

- 1/3 cup finely chopped onion
- 1 tablespoon butter
- 3 cups cubed day-old bread
- 1/4 teaspoon celery salt
- 1/4 teaspoon garlic powder
- 1/8 teaspoon salt
- 1/8 teaspoon pepper
- 1 egg, lightly beaten
- 10 bacon strips

In a small skillet, saute onion in butter until tender. In a large bowl, combine the bread cubes, celery salt, garlic powder, salt, pepper and onion mixture; toss to mix evenly. Add egg; toss to coat bread cubes. Roll mixture into ten 1-1/4-in. balls. Wrap a bacon strip around each ball. Secure bacon with a toothpick. Repeat with the remaining ingredients.

In a large skillet, cook bacon roll-ups on all sides over medium heat for 18 minutes or until bacon is crisp and a meat thermometer inserted into stuffing reads at least 160°. Drain on paper towels. **yield: 10 roll-ups.**

bacon roll-ups

coconut fried shrimp

Ann Atchison • O'Fallon, Missouri
These crunchy shrimp make a tempting starter or a fun change-of-pace main dish. The coconut coating adds a little sweetness…and the tangy orange marmalade and honey sauce combination is great for dipping. It's impossible to stop munching these once you start!

- 1-1/4 cups all-purpose flour
- 1-1/4 cups cornstarch
- 6-1/2 teaspoons baking powder
- 1/2 teaspoon salt
- 1/4 teaspoon Cajun seasoning
- 1-1/2 cups cold water
- 1/2 teaspoon canola oil
- 2-1/2 cups flaked coconut
- 1 pound uncooked large shrimp, peeled and deveined
- Additional oil for frying
- 1 cup orange marmalade
- 1/4 cup honey

In a small bowl, combine the first five ingredients. Stir in water and oil until smooth.

Place coconut in another bowl. Dip shrimp into batter, then coat with coconut. In an electric skillet or deep-fat fryer, heat oil to 375°. Fry shrimp, a few at a time, for 3 minutes or until golden brown. Drain on paper towels.

In a saucepan, heat marmalade and honey; stir until blended. Serve with shrimp. **yield: 4 servings.**

santa fe deviled eggs

In a small bowl, combine the cream cheese, crab and onion. Place 1 rounded teaspoonful in the center of each wonton wrapper. Moisten wrapper edges with water; fold in half lengthwise and press firmly to seal.

Keeping the filling in the center, again fold wonton wrapper lengthwise. Moisten the top of the short edges with water. Bring the two top edges from opposite sides together, overlapping the edges; press and seal (finished wonton resembles a nurse's hat).

In an electric skillet, heat 1 in. of oil to 375°. Fry the wontons for 1-2 minutes on each side or until golden brown. Drain the wontons on paper towels. Serve warm. **yield: 2 servings.**

santa fe deviled eggs

Patricia Harmon • Baden, Pennsylvania
I give my deviled eggs a zippy Southwestern flair. The smoky, spicy flavor is a hit with my husband, Paul.

> 2 hard-cooked eggs
> 1 tablespoon mayonnaise
> 1 tablespoon canned chopped green chilies
> 1/2 teaspoon chipotle pepper in adobo sauce
> 1/8 teaspoon garlic salt
> 4 teaspoons salsa
> 1 pitted ripe olive, quartered
> 1-1/2 teaspoons thinly sliced green onion

Cut eggs in half lengthwise. Remove yolks; set whites aside. In a small bowl, mash yolks. Stir in the mayonnaise, chilies, chipotle pepper and garlic salt. Stuff or pipe into egg whites.

Top with salsa, an olive piece and onion. Refrigerate until serving. **yield: 2 servings.**

creamy crab wontons

Robin Boynton • Harbor Beach, Michigan
How about a restaurant-style appetizer that's fast, too? These hot, crunchy little bites boast a rich, creamy filling with a hint of crab. They simply melt in your mouth. Serve wontons alongside plum sauce or sweet-and-sour sauce.

> 2 ounces cream cheese, softened
> 2 tablespoons canned crabmeat, drained, flaked and cartilage removed
> 2 teaspoons chopped green onion
> 6 wonton wrappers
Oil for frying

sausage cheese balls

Anna Damon • Bozeman, Montana
These bite-size meatballs are a favorite of mine. You can substitute your favorite cheese for the cheddar or serve the nibbles with Dijon mustard instead of barbecue sauce.

> 1/2 cup shredded cheddar cheese
> 3 tablespoons biscuit/baking mix
> 1 tablespoon finely chopped onion
> 1 tablespoon finely chopped celery
> 1/8 teaspoon garlic powder
> 1/8 teaspoon pepper
> 1/4 pound bulk pork sausage
Sweet-and-sour and barbecue sauce, optional

In a small bowl, combine the first six ingredients. Crumble sausage over mixture and mix well. Shape into 1-in. balls.

Place in a shallow baking pan coated with cooking spray. Bake, uncovered, at 375° for 12-15 minutes or until no longer pink. Drain on paper towels. Serve with sauces if desired. **yield: 1 dozen.**

sausage cheese balls

fresh tomato basil pizza

Jennifer Headlee • Baxter, Iowa

I crave this bruschetta-like pizza in spring, when I'm planting tomatoes in our garden. Slices make mouthwatering appetizers but you can also serve the bites alongside a grilled entree or as a meatless main course.

- 1 tube (8 ounces) refrigerated crescent rolls
- 2 garlic cloves, minced
- 1/2 cup chopped fresh basil
- 1 tablespoon olive oil
- 8 ounces sliced provolone cheese
- 4 medium tomatoes, thinly sliced
- 1/4 cup grated Parmesan cheese
- 1/4 teaspoon pepper

Unroll crescent dough into one long rectangle. Press into an ungreased 13-in. x 9-in. baking pan; seal seams and perforations. Bake at 375° for 14-16 minutes or until golden brown. Meanwhile, in a small skillet, saute garlic and basil in oil for 1 minute.

Arrange half of the provolone cheese over the crust. Layer with half of the tomatoes, basil mixture, Parmesan cheese and pepper. Repeat the layers. Bake pizza for 14-16 minutes or until the cheese is melted. **yield: 6 slices (3 servings).**

curried chicken tea sandwiches

Robin Fuhrman • Fond du Lac, Wisconsin

At the Victorian-theme bridal shower I hosted, I spread this dressed-up chicken salad on bread "hearts," but found it's also appealing served on a lettuce leaf. Chopped apples and dried cranberries add a splash of color and tang.

- 2 cups cubed cooked chicken
- 1 medium unpeeled red apple, chopped
- 3/4 cup dried cranberries
- 1/2 cup thinly sliced celery
- 1/4 cup chopped pecans
- 2 tablespoons thinly sliced green onions
- 3/4 cup mayonnaise
- 2 teaspoons lime juice
- 1/2 to 3/4 teaspoon curry powder
- 12 slices bread

Lettuce leaves

curried chicken tea sandwiches

In a large bowl, combine the first six ingredients. In a small bowl, combine the mayonnaise, lime juice and curry powder; pour over chicken mixture; toss to coat. Cover and refrigerate until ready to serve.

Cut each slice of bread with a 3-in. heart-shaped cookie cutter. Top bread slices with lettuce and chicken salad. **yield: 6 servings.**

cold vegetable pizza

Leslie Hampel • Palmer, Texas

Topped with a variety of crisp veggies, this great tasting pizza makes a cool first course on a warm day.

- 1 tube (4 ounces) refrigerated crescent rolls
- 1/4 cup mayonnaise
- 2 ounces cream cheese, softened
- 1/2 teaspoon dill weed
- 3/4 cup assorted chopped fresh vegetables (cucumber, radishes, red onion, green pepper *and/or* mushrooms)
- 2 tablespoons sliced ripe olives
- 3 tablespoons finely shredded cheddar cheese
- 3 tablespoons finely shredded part-skim mozzarella cheese

Unroll crescent rolls and place on an ungreased baking sheet. Flatten dough into an 8-in. x 5-in. rectangle. Seal seams and perforations. Bake at 375° for 10 minutes or until golden brown. Cool on a wire rack.

In a small bowl, combine mayonnaise, cream cheese and dill until blended; spread over crust. Top with vegetables of your choice. Sprinkle with olives and cheeses. Cover and chill at least 1 hour. Cut pizza into slices. Refrigerate leftovers. **yield: 4 servings.**

potato chip chicken strips

Sister Judith LaBrozzi • Canton, Ohio
This deliciously different spin on "chicken fingers" is a fast and tasty change from traditional fried chicken.

    1   cup (8 ounces) sour cream
  1/8   teaspoon garlic salt
  1/8   teaspoon onion salt
  1/8   teaspoon paprika
    1   package (12 ounces) potato chips, crushed
    2   pounds boneless skinless chicken breasts, cut into 1-inch strips
  1/4   cup butter, melted
Salsa, barbecue sauce *or* sweet-and-sour sauce

In a shallow bowl, combine sour cream and seasonings. Place crushed potato chips in another shallow bowl. Dip chicken strips in sour cream mixture, then coat with potato chips. Place in a greased 15-in. x 10-in. x 1-in. baking pan. Drizzle with butter.

Bake at 400° for 20-22 minutes or until chicken is no longer pink. Serve the chicken strips with salsa or sauce. **yield: 6 main-dish or 10 appetizer servings.**

tomato basil snackers

Taste of Home Test Kitchen
Fresh basil, summer-ripe tomatoes and melted mozzarella top toasted English muffins in this fabulous afternoon pick-me-up.

    2   English muffins, split and toasted
    2   tablespoons fat-free mayonnaise

tomato basil snackers

pecan cheddar snacks

    3   plum tomatoes, cut into 1/4-inch slices
    6   fresh basil leaves, thinly sliced
  1/8   teaspoon pepper
  1/2   cup shredded part-skim mozzarella cheese

Place English muffin halves on an ungreased baking sheet; spread with mayonnaise. Top muffin halves with the tomatoes, basil, pepper and cheese. Broil 4 in. from the heat for 3-4 minutes or until the cheese is melted. **yield: 4 servings.**

pecan cheddar snacks

Nellie Webb • Athens, Tennessee
Once you take a bite of these crisp and chewy cheese balls, you'll surely want more. I make them for the holidays and other special occasions, and I keep some in the freezer so they're ready to serve anytime.

  1/2   cup all-purpose flour
    1   tablespoon biscuit/baking mix
Pinch cayenne pepper
  1/4   cup butter, softened
  1/2   cup shredded cheddar cheese
    1   egg, beaten
    1   cup crisp rice cereal
  1/2   cup chopped pecans

In a bowl, combine the flour, biscuit mix and cayenne. Stir in butter until crumbly. Add cheese and egg; mix well. Stir in cereal and pecans.

Shape into 1-1/2-in. balls; place on an ungreased baking sheet. Bake at 350° for 18-20 minutes or until lightly browned. Serve warm. **yield: 2-3 servings.**

honey-orange chicken wings

Marie Schnerch
Winnipeg, Manitoba
These wings were my
mom's recipe. She served
them hot as a main dish,
but my dad loved them
cold. I like to serve them as
an appetizer, hot or cold.

honey-orange chicken wings

6	**whole chicken wings**
1/3	**cup ketchup**
1/2	**cup all-purpose flour**
3	**tablespoons orange juice**
4-1/2	**teaspoons honey**
3/4	**teaspoon lemon juice**
3/4	**teaspoon Worcestershire sauce**
1/8	**teaspoon ground ginger**

Dash garlic powder

Cut chicken wings into three sections; discard wing tip sections. Brush wings with ketchup; coat with flour. Place in a shallow baking pan coated with cooking spray. Bake, uncovered, at 350° for 20 minutes.

In a small bowl, combine the remaining ingredients. Brush some of the mixture over wings. Bake 15-20 minutes longer or until chicken juices run clear, basting frequently with remaining orange juice mixture. **yield: 2 servings.**

cheesy tenderloin strips

Marjorie Miller • Haven, Kansas
My mother-in-law originally made this recipe with chicken. When I substituted pork and made several other revisions, my family reveled in the delicious results! It's simple to prepare yet so very tasty.

  3 tablespoons butter, melted
1/4 cup crushed butter-flavored crackers
  3 tablespoons finely shredded cheddar cheese
  2 tablespoons grated Parmesan cheese
1/2 teaspoon dried basil
1/4 teaspoon salt
1/4 teaspoon pepper
  1 pork tenderloin (1/2 pound), cut into 1/2-inch slices
Marinara sauce, warmed, optional

Place butter in a shallow bowl. In another shallow bowl, combine the crackers crumbs, cheeses, basil, salt and pepper. Dip pork in butter, then roll in crumb mixture. Place on an ungreased foil-lined baking sheet. Bake at 400° for 10-15 minutes or until juices run clear. Serve with marinara sauce if desired. **yield: 2 servings.**

cheesy tenderloin strips

tomato tart with three cheeses

Taste of Home Test Kitchen
This quick and easy recipe from our home economists will delight the pizza lovers in your home. You'll be surprised at how effortless it is.

  1 sheet frozen puff pastry, thawed
3/4 cup shredded part-skim mozzarella cheese
3/4 cup shredded provolone cheese
1/4 cup minced fresh basil
  4 plum tomatoes, thinly sliced
Salt and pepper to taste
1/4 cup shredded Parmesan cheese
Additional minced fresh basil

Unfold pastry sheet on a lightly floured surface. Roll into a 12-in. square; transfer to a parchment paper-lined baking sheet. Prick with a fork.

Combine the mozzarella, provolone and basil; sprinkle over the pastry to within 1 in. of edges. Arrange the tomato slices over the cheese. Season with salt and pepper; sprinkle with Parmesan cheese.

Bake at 400° for 15-20 minutes or until pastry is golden brown. Remove tart from baking sheet to a wire rack to cool for 5 minutes. Sprinkle with additional basil. Cut into slices. Serve the slices hot or at room temperature. **yield: 4 servings.**

sloppy joe nachos

Janet Rhoden • Hortonville, Wisconsin
When my kids were little, they loved these snacks because they could eat with their fingers. The nachos make an irresistible speedy meal, tailgate food or party staple.

  1 pound ground beef
  1 can (15-1/2 ounces) sloppy joe sauce
  1 package (12 ounces) tortilla chips
3/4 cup shredded cheddar cheese
1/4 cup sliced ripe olives, optional

In a large skillet, cook beef over medium heat until no longer pink; drain. Add the sloppy joe sauce; cook, uncovered, for 5 minutes or until heated through.

Arrange tortilla chips on a serving plate. Top with meat mixture, cheese and olives if desired. **yield: 6 servings.**

soups & sandwiches

Sized right for a duo, these satisfying soups and sandwiches make quite a pair. The classic dishes we've selected will fill you up without packing the fridge with extra food.

autumn chowder, page 52

Jeanne Holt
Saint Paul, Minnesota
These burgers are my way of enjoying the flavors of Buffalo chicken wings while avoiding some of the fat and calories that go with them.

buffalo chicken burgers with tangy slaw

SLAW:
- 1/4 cup thinly sliced celery
- 1/4 cup shredded apple
- 2 tablespoons fat-free blue cheese salad dressing
- 1 teaspoon finely chopped walnuts

SAUCE:
- 3 tablespoons Louisiana-style hot sauce
- 2 teaspoons ketchup
- 2 teaspoons reduced-fat butter, melted

BURGERS:
- 2 tablespoons chopped sweet red pepper
- 2 tablespoons plus 4 teaspoons thinly sliced green onions, *divided*
- 1 tablespoon unsweetened applesauce
- 1/4 teaspoon salt
- 1/4 teaspoon garlic salt
- 1/4 teaspoon pepper
- 1 pound ground chicken
- 4 lettuce leaves
- 4 hamburger buns, split

In a small bowl, combine the celery, apple, salad dressing and walnuts. In another small bowl, combine the Louisiana-style hot sauce, ketchup and butter; set aside.

In a large bowl, combine the red pepper, 2 tablespoons green onion, applesauce, salt, garlic salt and pepper. Crumble chicken over mixture and mix well. Shape into four burgers.

Broil 6 in. from the heat for 5-7 minutes on each side or until a meat thermometer reads 165° and juices run clear, basting occasionally with reserved sauce. Serve burgers on lettuce-lined buns; top each with 2 tablespoons slaw. Sprinkle with remaining green onions and replace bun tops. **yield: 4 servings.**

Editor's Note: This recipe was tested with Land O'Lakes light stick butter.

creamy spring soup

Dora Handy • Alliance, Ohio

At the end of a long day, there's nothing better than enjoying a bowl of this warm, creamy soup. It comes together in a flash, and with so many fresh, delicious veggies, it's full of the vitamins we all don't get enough of.

- 1 can (14-1/2 ounces) reduced-sodium chicken broth
- 4 fresh asparagus spears, trimmed and cut into 2-inch pieces
- 4 baby carrots, julienned
- 1/2 celery rib, chopped
- 1 green onion, chopped
- Dash garlic powder
- Dash pepper
- 3/4 cup cooked elbow macaroni
- 1 can (5-1/2 ounces) evaporated milk
- 3/4 cup fresh baby spinach

In a large saucepan, combine the first seven ingredients. Bring to a boil. Reduce heat; cover and simmer for 5 minutes or until the vegetables are tender. Stir in the cooked macaroni, evaporated milk and spinach; heat through. **yield: 2 servings.**

gouda turkey club

creamy spring soup

gouda turkey club

Karen Harris • Castle Rock, Colorado

With this recipe, two can enjoy the taste of something new and elegant in minutes. All you need to add is a little ambiance for a bistro meal at home.

- 1/2 cup shredded smoked Gouda cheese
- 4-1/2 teaspoons mayonnaise
- 1 tablespoon thinly sliced green onion
- 1/4 teaspoon garlic powder
- 1/4 teaspoon coarsely ground pepper
- 4 slices whole wheat bread, crusts removed and toasted
- 2 teaspoons butter, softened
- 1/4 pound shaved deli hickory smoked turkey
- 4 slices tomato
- 1/2 medium ripe avocado, peeled and mashed
- 2 romaine leaves

In a small bowl, combine the cheese, mayonnaise, onion, garlic powder and pepper. Spread two slices of toast with butter; layer with cheese mixture, turkey, tomato, avocado and romaine. Top with remaining toast. Cut each sandwich in half. **yield: 2 servings.**

simple minestrone

Regina Cook • Fort Worth, Texas
I can make this classic recipe extra quickly for a cool winter night. The timeless soup is chock-full of vegetables and has a wonderful smoky flavor.

- 1   bacon strip, diced
- 1/3 cup smoked turkey kielbasa, quartered
- 1   small onion, chopped
- 1   garlic clove, minced
- 1/4 cup chopped carrot
- 2   tablespoons chopped celery
- 1   cup reduced-sodium chicken broth
- 1   cup canned diced tomatoes, undrained
- 1   can (5-1/2 ounces) reduced-sodium tomato juice
- 1/4 cup chopped zucchini
- 1/2 teaspoon dried basil
- 1/4 teaspoon dried oregano
- 1/8 teaspoon pepper
- 1/3 cup canned pinto beans, rinsed and drained
- 1/4 cup cooked elbow macaroni
- 1   tablespoon grated Parmesan cheese

In a large saucepan, cook bacon over medium heat until crisp. Using a slotted spoon, remove the bacon to paper towel. In the drippings, saute sausage, onion and garlic for 3 minutes. Stir in the carrot and celery. Cook and stir 2 minutes longer or until the sausage is lightly browned; drain.

Stir in the broth, tomatoes, tomato juice, zucchini and seasonings. Bring to a boil. Reduce heat; cover and simmer for 10 minutes or until vegetables are tender. Stir in the beans and macaroni; heat through. Sprinkle with Parmesan cheese and bacon. **yield: 2 servings.**

simple minestrone

lemon-chicken velvet soup

lemon-chicken velvet soup

Celeste Buckley • Redding, California
The lively flavor of lemon perks up this rich, brothy soup accented with sugar snap peas. I enjoy this soup with a green salad, sourdough bread and a glass of white wine.

- 2   tablespoons butter
- 2   tablespoons all-purpose flour
- 1   can (14-1/2 ounces) chicken broth
- 3   tablespoons lemon juice
- 1-1/2 cups cubed cooked chicken breast
- 10   fresh *or* frozen sugar snap peas
- 2   tablespoons minced fresh parsley
- 1   teaspoon grated lemon peel
- 3   tablespoons heavy whipping cream

In a small saucepan, melt butter. Stir in the flour until smooth; gradually add broth and lemon juice. Bring to a boil; cook and stir for 1-2 minutes or until thickened.

Stir in the chicken, peas, parsley and lemon peel; cook 2-3 minutes longer or until chicken is heated through and peas are crisp-tender. Stir in cream; heat through (do not boil). **yield: 2 servings.**

spinach pastrami wraps

Rhonda Wilkinson • Levittown, Pennsylvania
I get frequent requests for these hearty, flavorful wraps. They can be sliced and served for appetizers as well.

4	flour tortillas (10 inches), room temperature
4	ounces cream cheese, softened
3/4	cup shredded cheddar cheese
1/4	cup chopped red onion
1/4	cup sliced Greek olives
1/2	pound thinly sliced deli pastrami
1-1/2	cups fresh baby spinach

Spread tortillas with cream cheese; sprinkle with cheddar cheese, onion and olives. Top with pastrami and spinach. Roll up tightly; secure with toothpicks. **yield: 4 servings.**

onion soup with sausage

Sundra Hauck • Bogalusa, Louisiana
With a yummy slice of mozzarella cheese bread broiled on top, this robust broth makes an impressive luncheon or light supper. It looks great and tastes wonderful.

1/2	pound pork sausage links, cut into 1/2-inch pieces
1	pound sliced fresh mushrooms
1	cup sliced onion
2	cans (14-1/2 ounces *each*) beef broth
4	slices Italian bread
1/2	cup shredded part-skim mozzarella cheese

In a large saucepan, cook sausage over medium heat until no longer pink; drain. Add mushrooms and onion; cook for 4-6 minutes or until tender. Stir in the broth. Bring to a boil. Reduce heat; simmer, uncovered, for 4-6 minutes or until heated through.

Ladle into four 2-cup ovenproof bowls. Top each with a slice of bread; sprinkle with cheese. Broil until cheese is melted. **yield: 4 servings.**

hot ham 'n' cheese sandwiches

Kathy Taylor • Mason City, Iowa
These mouthwatering sandwiches are so fast and hassle-free that we end up eating them quite often. They're perfect when you're heading out the door or getting home late.

2	tablespoons mayonnaise
2	kaiser rolls, split
1/4	cup shredded cheddar cheese
4	slices cooked bacon strips
6	slices deli ham (1/2 ounce *each*)
1/4	cup shredded part-skim mozzarella cheese

Spread mayonnaise over rolls. Layer roll bottoms with cheddar cheese, bacon, ham and mozzarella cheese; replace tops. Wrap sandwiches in foil; place on an ungreased baking sheet.

Bake at 350° for 15-20 minutes or until cheese is melted. **yield: 2 servings.**

rocky ford chili

rocky ford chili

Karen Golden • Phoenix, Arizona

When my brother and sister were in grade school in little Rocky Ford, Colorado, this comforting chili dish was served in the school cafeteria. My siblings described it to my mother so she could duplicate it at home. We all enjoy preparing it for our own families now.

 2 cans (14.3 ounces *each*) chili with beans
 1 package (10 ounces) frozen corn
 4 cups corn chips
 1 cup shredded lettuce
 1 cup (4 ounces) shredded Mexican cheese blend
 1 can (2-1/4 ounces) sliced ripe olives, drained
 1/4 cup sour cream
 1/4 cup salsa

In a large microwave-safe bowl, cook chili and corn on high for 2-4 minutes or until heated through. Place corn chips in four large soup bowls; top with chili mixture, lettuce, cheese, olives, sour cream and salsa. **yield: 4 servings.**

Editor's Note: This recipe was tested in a 1,100-watt microwave.

hearty cheese soup

Suzanna Snader • Fredericksburg, Pennsylvania

Thick and creamy, this pleasing soup is bubbling with the taste of rich cheese. Several years ago, I came home with this recipe after an exchange at my church, and I have shared it with many people since then.

1-1/2 cups cubed peeled potatoes
 1/2 cup water
 1/4 cup sliced celery
 1/4 cup sliced fresh carrots
 2 tablespoons chopped onion
 1/2 teaspoon chicken bouillon granules
 1/2 teaspoon dried parsley flakes
 1/4 teaspoon salt
Dash pepper
1-1/2 teaspoons all-purpose flour
 3/4 cup milk
 1/4 pound process cheese (Velveeta), cubed

In a small saucepan, combine the first nine ingredients. Bring to a boil. Reduce heat; cover and simmer for 10-12 minutes or until potatoes are tender.

In a small bowl, combine flour and milk until smooth. Stir into vegetable mixture. Bring to a boil; cook and stir for 2 minutes or until thickened. Reduce heat to low; stir in cheese until melted. **yield: 2 servings.**

grilled pepper jack chicken sandwiches

Linda Foreman • Locust Grove, Oklahoma

These big bites make a great main dish for summer cookouts. Basic, yet packed with flavor, the sandwich gets a kick from zesty cheese and smoky, savory bacon.

 2 boneless skinless chicken breast halves (4 ounces *each*)
 1 teaspoon poultry seasoning
 2 center-cut bacon strips, cooked and halved
 2 slices (1/2 ounce *each*) pepper Jack cheese
 2 hamburger buns, split
 2 lettuce leaves
 1 slice onion, separated into rings
 2 slices tomato
Dill pickle slices, optional

Sprinkle the chicken with poultry seasoning. Using long-handled tongs, moisten a paper towel with cooking oil and lightly coat the grill rack.

Grill chicken, covered, over medium heat or broil 4 in. from the heat for 4-7 minutes on each side or until a meat thermometer reads 170°. Top chicken with bacon and cheese; cover and grill 1-2 minutes longer or until cheese is melted.

Serve on buns with lettuce, onion, tomato and pickles if desired. **yield: 2 servings.**

cooking tip
2

Want an effortless way to add flavor and texture to your soups? Try this! Drop small scoops of boxed stuffing mix into boiling soup. The stuffing turns into tender and perfectly seasoned dumplings.

Michael Cohen
Los Angeles,
California
Take flatbreads smothered with pesto, wrap them around steak and top with cheese, and you have an instant party! Guests will love the fun presentation and the mouthwatering taste.

tuscan steak flatbreads

SUN-DRIED TOMATO PESTO:
- 1/3 cup packed fresh parsley sprigs
- 2 tablespoons fresh basil leaves
- 1 garlic clove, quartered
- 2 tablespoons grated Parmesan cheese
- 2 tablespoons oil-packed sun-dried tomatoes, patted dry
- 2 tablespoons sherry
- 1/4 teaspoon salt

Dash pepper
- 1/4 cup olive oil

STEAK FLATBREADS:
- 1 beef top sirloin steak (3/4 inch thick and 1-1/4 pounds)
- 1/4 teaspoon salt
- 1/4 teaspoon pepper
- 4 flatbreads *or* whole pita breads

- 2 tablespoons olive oil
- 1 cup (4 ounces) shredded fontina cheese
- 1/4 cup fresh basil leaves, thinly sliced

For pesto, place the parsley, basil and garlic in a food processor; cover and pulse until chopped. Add the Parmesan cheese, tomatoes, sherry, salt and pepper; cover and process until blended. While processing, gradually add oil in a steady stream. Set aside.

Sprinkle steak with salt and pepper. Grill, covered, over medium heat for 6-10 minutes on each side or until meat reaches desired doneness (for medium-rare, a meat thermometer should read 145°; medium, 160°; well-done, 170°). Remove and keep warm.

Brush one side of each flatbread with oil; place oiled side down on grill rack. Grill, covered, over medium heat for 1-2 minutes or until the flatbread is heated through.

Spread pesto over grilled side of flatbreads. Cut steak into thin strips; place over pesto. Top with fontina cheese and basil. **yield: 4 servings.**

golden asparagus soup

Heather Ahrens • Avon, Ohio

It doesn't matter how many times I serve this thick, buttery soup, it's always a hit. It's a springtime classic and a great way to get your daily veggies.

    3/4   pound fresh asparagus, trimmed
    1/2   cup chopped onion
      2   tablespoons butter
      2   garlic cloves, minced
      1   cup thinly sliced carrots
      1   can (14-1/2 ounces) chicken broth
    1/4   cup minced fresh parsley
      1   tablespoon minced fresh basil
    1/4   teaspoon salt
    1/4   teaspoon pepper

Cut tips off asparagus and set aside; cut the stalks into 1-1/2-in. pieces. In a large saucepan, saute onion in butter until tender. Add garlic; cook 1 minute longer. Add carrots and asparagus; cook for 2 minutes.

Stir in the broth, parsley, basil, salt and pepper. Bring to a boil. Reduce heat; cover and simmer for 20-25 minutes or until vegetables are tender. Cool slightly.

In a blender, cover and process soup until blended. Return to pan. Stir in asparagus tips; cook for 8-10 minutes or until tender. **yield: 2 servings.**

egg salad burritos

golden asparagus soup

egg salad burritos

Sarah Inglis • Wappingers Falls, New York

I visited Mexico last year and was inspired by the fresh flavor of the food. Tomatillos and limes were widely used, and they add a tangy punch to this egg salad.

      4   hard-cooked eggs, chopped
    1/4   cup mayonnaise
      2   teaspoons minced fresh cilantro
      1   tablespoon lime juice
    1/4   teaspoon cayenne pepper, optional
    1/8   teaspoon salt
    Dash pepper
      2   whole wheat tortillas (8 inches)
      1   medium tomato, thinly sliced
      1   medium tomatillo, husks removed, rinsed and thinly sliced

In a small bowl, combine the eggs, mayonnaise, cilantro, lime juice, cayenne if desired, salt and pepper. Layer tortillas with tomato, tomatillo and egg salad mixture. Fold sides and ends over filling and roll up. **yield: 2 servings.**

beefstro bruschetta burgers

Grill or broil bread for 1-2 minutes on each side or until toasted. Spread each slice of toast with 1-1/4 teaspoons reserved mustard sauce. Layer each with arugula, a burger, a cheese slice and 1-1/4 teaspoons additional sauce. Garnish with peppers and prosciutto. Serve immediately. **yield: 4 servings.**

cranberry chicken salad sandwiches

Michaela Rosenthal • Woodland Hills, California
Scrumptious and filling, this is a great way to use up leftover cranberry sauce. It really brightens the flavor.

    2   sandwich buns, split
    2   teaspoons butter, softened
    2   teaspoons cream cheese, softened
    1   cup shredded cooked chicken
  1/3   cup whole-berry cranberry sauce
    3   tablespoons mayonnaise
    2   green onions, chopped
    1   teaspoon lemon juice
    2   lettuce leaves

Place buns cut side up on an ungreased baking sheet. Spread butter over bun bottoms. Broil 3-4 in. from the heat for 1-2 minutes or until golden brown. Spread cream cheese on bun tops.

In a small bowl, combine the chicken, cranberry sauce, mayonnaise, onions and lemon juice. Spread over bun bottoms. Top each with a lettuce leaf; replace tops. **yield: 2 servings.**

beefstro bruschetta burgers

Devon Delaney • Princeton, New Jersey
My mom always put her hamburger on top of a salad. I thought it was quite unusual as a child, but I adjusted the concept to make it a light and tasty meal for the whole family!

    3   tablespoons Dijon mustard
    3   tablespoons reduced-sugar apricot preserves
    1   tablespoon prepared horseradish
    2   thin slices prosciutto *or* deli ham, chopped
    1   pound lean ground beef (90% lean)
  3/4   teaspoon salt-free lemon-pepper seasoning
    8   slices French bread (1/2 inch thick)
    1   cup fresh arugula *or* baby spinach
    2   ounces Brie cheese, cut into eight thin slices
  1/4   cup julienned roasted sweet red peppers

In a small bowl, combine the mustard, preserves and horseradish. In a small skillet coated with cooking spray, cook and stir prosciutto over medium heat until lightly browned. Set aside.

In a large bowl, combine the ground beef and lemon-pepper seasoning. Shape into eight patties.

Using long-handled tongs, moisten a paper towel with cooking oil and lightly coat the grill rack. Grill burgers, covered, over medium heat or broil 4 in. from heat for 3-4 minutes on each side until a meat thermometer reads 160° and juices run clear. Remove the burgers and keep warm.

cranberry chicken salad sandwiches

potato vegetable soup

garden fresh subs

Mary Ann Dell • Phoenixville, Pennsylvania
This wonderful summer recipe came from a friend. With a variety of classic veggie favorites, it makes for a quick bite. These piled-high sandwiches are sure to be a hit.

3	tablespoons sour cream
1/2	teaspoon Italian seasoning

Dash garlic salt

2	French rolls, split
2	lettuce leaves
4	thin slices hard salami (1/4 ounce *each*)
2	slices process American cheese (3/4 ounce *each*)
1	slice Swiss cheese (3/4 ounce), halved
4	slices tomato
8	thin cucumber slices
4	green pepper rings
2	tablespoons sliced ripe olives
2	tablespoons thinly sliced green onions

In a small bowl, combine the sour cream, Italian seasoning and garlic salt. Spread over rolls. Layer the remaining ingredients on roll bottoms. Replace tops. **yield: 2 servings.**

potato vegetable soup

Jan Hancock • Evansville, Wisconsin
Comforting and chock-full of colorful veggies, this thick, chowder-like soup makes cozy fare. Pair it with freshly baked bread, and it's a meal by itself.

1	bacon strip, diced
1	medium potato, peeled and cubed
1/2	medium carrot, sliced
1/2	cup water
2	tablespoons chopped celery
2	tablespoons chopped onion
1/4	teaspoon salt
1/8	teaspoon pepper
1	tablespoon all-purpose flour
1	cup 2% milk
1/4	cup shredded cheddar cheese
2	teaspoons butter

In a small saucepan, cook bacon over medium heat until crisp. Using a slotted spoon, remove to paper towels; drain. In the same pan, combine the potato, carrot, water, celery, onion, salt and pepper. Bring to a boil. Reduce heat; cover and simmer for 15 minutes or until vegetables are tender.

In a small bowl, combine flour and milk until smooth; stir into vegetable mixture. Bring to a boil; cook and stir for 2 minutes or until thickened. Reduce heat. Add cheese and butter; stir until cheese is melted. Garnish with bacon. **yield: 2 servings.**

garden fresh subs

gingered pumpkin bisque

Patricia Kile • Elizabethtown, Pennsylvania
Every spoonful of this pretty pumpkin soup hints of autumn.
Serve it as the first course at special sit-down dinners.

1/3	cup chopped shallots
1/4	cup chopped onion
1	teaspoon minced fresh gingerroot
1	tablespoon canola oil
2	tablespoons all-purpose flour
1	can (14-1/2 ounces) chicken broth
1/3	cup apple cider *or* juice
3/4	cup plus 2 tablespoons canned pumpkin
2	tablespoons plus 1-1/2 teaspoons maple syrup
1/8	teaspoon dried thyme
1/8	teaspoon ground cinnamon
1/8	teaspoon pepper

Dash ground cloves

1/2	cup heavy whipping cream *or* half-and-half cream
1/4	teaspoon vanilla extract

Additional heavy whipping cream, optional
Fresh thyme sprigs, optional

In a small saucepan, saute the shallots, onion and ginger in oil until tender. Stir in flour until blended; cook and stir for 2 minutes or until golden brown. Gradually stir in broth and cider. Bring to a boil; cook and stir for 2 minutes or until thickened.

Stir in pumpkin, syrup and seasonings. Return to a boil. Reduce heat. Cover; simmer for 10 minutes. Remove from heat; cool slightly. In a blender, process soup in batches until smooth. Return all to pan. Stir in cream and vanilla; heat through (do not boil). If desired, drizzle servings with additional cream and garnish with thyme. **yield: 4 servings.**

gingered pumpkin bisque

ranch turkey wraps

Emily Hanson • Logan, Utah
These handheld favorites make for a nice lunch or a quick dinner on the go. A great thing about wraps is that, like sandwiches, you can customize each one with ingredients to suit your family members' different tastes.

1/4	cup cream cheese, softened
1/4	cup prepared ranch salad dressing
4	flour tortillas (10 inches), warmed
3/4	pound sliced deli turkey
8	slices Monterey Jack cheese
1	medium ripe avocado, peeled and sliced
1	medium tomato, sliced

In a small bowl, beat cream cheese and salad dressing until smooth. Spread over tortillas. Layer with turkey, cheese, avocado and tomato. Roll up tightly; cut in half. **yield: 4 servings.**

super grilled cheese sandwiches

Debbie Murray • Ft. Worth, Texas
Heat up your indoor grill to make this ooey-gooey grilled cheese sandwich recipe. They're delicious served with soup!

4	slices Italian bread
2	slices (3/4 ounce *each*) Muenster cheese
2	slices (3/4 ounce *each*) Swiss cheese
2	slices (3/4 ounce *each*) process American cheese
2	slices (3/4 ounce *each*) part-skim mozzarella cheese
1	tablespoon butter, softened
1/4	teaspoon garlic salt with parsley

On two slices of bread, layer the cheeses; top with remaining bread. Butter the outsides of sandwiches; sprinkle with garlic salt.

Cook on an indoor grill or panini maker for 1-2 minutes or until the bread is browned and the cheese is melted. **yield: 2 servings.**

cooking tip 2

With its slightly sharp flavor, cilantro gives a distinctive taste to Mexican, Latin American and Asian dishes. Like all other fresh herbs, cilantro should be used as soon as possible. For short-term storage, immerse the freshly cut stems in water about 2 inches deep. Cover loosely with a plastic bag and refrigerate.

Carolyn Phenicie
Titusville,
Pennsylvania
I tried this sandwich while vacationing in Sedona, Arizona, and I fell in love with it. When I returned home, I developed this version, which tastes just like the original.

grilled veggie sandwiches with cilantro pesto

- 2/3 **cup packed fresh cilantro sprigs**
- 1/4 **cup packed fresh parsley sprigs**
- 2 **tablespoons grated Parmesan cheese**
- 2 **garlic cloves, peeled**
- 2 **tablespoons water**
- 1 **tablespoon pine nuts**
- 1 **tablespoon olive oil**
- **Cooking spray**
- 2 **large sweet red peppers**
- 4 **slices eggplant (1/2 inch thick)**
- 1/2 **teaspoon salt**
- 1/4 **teaspoon pepper**
- 1/2 **cup shredded part-skim mozzarella cheese**
- 4 **hard rolls, split**

For pesto, place the cilantro, parsley, Parmesan cheese and garlic in a small food processor; cover and pulse until chopped. Add water and pine nuts; cover and process until well blended. While processing, gradually add oil in a steady stream. Set aside.

Using long-handled tongs, moisten a paper towel with cooking oil and lightly coat the grill rack. Grill peppers over medium heat for 10-15 minutes or until the skins blister, turning frequently.

Immediately place the peppers in a large bowl; cover and let stand for 15-20 minutes. Peel off and discard charred skin. Halve and seed peppers; set aside.

Lightly coat eggplant on both sides with cooking spray; sprinkle with salt and pepper. Grill, covered, over medium heat for 3-5 minutes on each side or until tender.

Top each eggplant slice with a pepper half; sprinkle with mozzarella cheese. Grill, covered, for 2-3 minutes or until cheese is melted. Spread each roll with 1 tablespoon reserved pesto; top each with an eggplant stack. Replace roll tops. **yield: 4 servings.**

creamy wild rice soup

creamy wild rice soup

Marilyn Ausland • Columbus, Georgia

My husband and I call this our favorite soup—it never gets old! It's creamy, comforting and perfect on chilly days.

- 1/4 cup chopped onion
- 1/4 cup thinly sliced celery
- 1/4 cup sliced fresh mushrooms
- 1 green onion, thinly sliced
- 1/4 cup reduced-fat butter
- 1/4 cup all-purpose flour
- 1/8 teaspoon pepper
- 1 can (14-1/2 ounces) reduced-sodium chicken broth
- 1 cup cooked wild rice
- 1/4 cup diced fully cooked lean ham
- 1-1/2 teaspoons diced pimientos
- 1/2 cup fat-free half-and-half
- 1 tablespoon sliced almonds, toasted, optional

In a large saucepan, saute onion, celery, mushrooms and green onion in butter until tender. Stir in flour and pepper until blended. Gradually stir in broth. Bring to a boil. Cook; stir for 1-2 minutes. Reduce heat. Stir in rice, ham and pimientos; heat through. Stir in half-and-half; heat through (do not boil). Sprinkle with almonds if desired. **yield: 3 servings.**

turkey salad on wheat

Merrijane Rice • Bountiful, Utah

Simple yet filling, this is a delightful twist on turkey salad. Green onions and bacon give it a sweet-and-savory taste.

- 2/3 cup chopped romaine
- 1/2 cup diced cooked turkey
- 2 tablespoons shredded Swiss cheese
- 1 green onion, thinly sliced
- 2 bacon strips, cooked and crumbled
- 2 tablespoons frozen peas, thawed
- 3 tablespoons mayonnaise

Dash pepper
- 4 slices whole wheat bread

In a small bowl, combine the first six ingredients. Stir in mayonnaise and pepper. Spread over two slices of bread; top with remaining bread. **yield: 2 servings.**

spinach cheese soup

Maria Regakis • Somerville, Massachusetts

Give yourself a delicious calcium boost with this velvety, cheesy soup. I like to serve it with a green salad. You can also add 2 cups of cubed cooked chicken, if you wish.

- 1 cup chicken broth
- 1 package (6 ounces) fresh baby spinach, chopped
- 1/2 teaspoon onion powder
- 1/8 teaspoon pepper
- 4 teaspoons all-purpose flour
- 1 can (5 ounces) evaporated milk
- 1 cup (4 ounces) shredded cheddar cheese

In a small saucepan, combine the broth, spinach, onion powder and pepper. Bring to a boil. Combine flour and milk until smooth; gradually add to soup. Return to a boil. Reduce heat; cook and stir for 2 minutes or until thickened. Stir in cheese until melted. **yield: 2 servings.**

spinach cheese soup

cobb salad sandwiches

cobb salad sandwiches

Taste of Home Test Kitchen
Satisfy the whole family with a sandwich version of the classic salad. It's easy to customize them to suit each person's tastes.

- 1/4 **cup mayonnaise**
- 1/2 **teaspoon prepared horseradish**
- 1/4 **teaspoon dried basil**
- 4 **croissants, split**
- 4 **lettuce leaves**
- 1 **medium tomato, sliced**
- 4 **cooked bacon strips, halved**
- 4 **slices deli ham**
- 3 **hard-cooked eggs, sliced**

In a small bowl, combine the mayonnaise, horseradish and basil; spread over cut side of croissant bottoms. Layer with lettuce, tomato, bacon, ham and eggs; replace tops. **yield: 4 servings.**

chicken tortilla soup

Kathy Averbeck • Dousman, Wisconsin
Showcasing a variety of vegetables and autumn color, this soup is ideal for using up fresh garden bounty. Add richness to the flavor by first grilling the chicken and vegetables.

- 2 **medium tomatoes**
- 1 **small onion, cut into wedges**
- 1 **garlic clove, peeled**
- 4 **teaspoons canola oil,** *divided*
- 1 **boneless skinless chicken breast half (6 ounces)**
- 1/4 **teaspoon lemon-pepper seasoning**
- 1/8 **teaspoon salt**
- 2 **corn tortillas (6 inches)**

- 1/2 **cup diced zucchini**
- 2 **tablespoons chopped carrot**
- 1 **tablespoon minced fresh cilantro**
- 3/4 **teaspoon ground cumin**
- 1/2 **teaspoon chili powder**
- 1 **cup reduced-sodium chicken broth**
- 1/2 **cup spicy hot V8 juice**
- 1/3 **cup frozen corn**
- 2 **tablespoons tomato puree**
- 1-1/2 **teaspoons chopped seeded jalapeno pepper**
- 1 **bay leaf**
- 1/4 **cup cubed** *or* **sliced avocado**
- 1/4 **cup shredded Mexican cheese blend**

Brush the tomatoes, onion and garlic with 1 teaspoon oil. Broil 4 in. from the heat for 3-4 minutes on each side or until tender. Peel and discard charred skin from tomatoes; place in a blender. Add onion and garlic; cover and process for 1-2 minutes or until smooth.

Sprinkle the chicken with lemon-pepper and salt; broil for 5-6 minutes on each side or until a meat thermometer reads 170°. Cut one tortilla into 1/4-in. strips; coarsely chop remaining tortilla.

In a large saucepan, heat remaining oil. Fry tortilla strips until crisp and browned; remove with a slotted spoon.

In the same pan, cook the zucchini, carrot, cilantro, cumin, chili powder and chopped tortilla over medium heat for 4 minutes. Stir in tomato mixture, broth, juice, corn, puree, jalapeno and bay leaf. Bring to a boil. Reduce heat. Simmer, uncovered, for 20 minutes.

Cut chicken into strips; add to soup. Simmer 5 minutes longer or until chicken is no longer pink. Discard bay leaf. Garnish with the avocado, cheese and tortilla strips. **yield: 3-1/2 cups.**

Editor's Note: When cutting hot peppers, disposable gloves are recommended. Avoid touching your face.

chicken tortilla soup

grilled cheese & pepper sandwiches

Arline Hofland • Deer Lodge, Montana
This is a wholesome sandwich to make for one or two. It's a nice twist on traditional grilled cheese. It's so filling and especially good with rye bread!

4	slices rye bread with caraway seeds
2	tablespoons butter, softened, *divided*
1/2	cup chopped onion
1/2	cup chopped green pepper
1/2	cup chopped sweet red pepper
2	teaspoons chopped seeded jalapeno pepper
2	tablespoons olive oil
3/4	cup shredded Monterey Jack cheese

Butter one side of each slice of rye bread with 1/2 teaspoon butter; set aside. In a small skillet, saute onion and peppers in oil until tender. Spoon onto two bread slices; top with cheese and remaining bread. Spread outsides of sandwiches with remaining butter.

In a large skillet, toast sandwiches for 3 minutes on each side or until golden brown. **yield: 2 servings.**

Editor's Note: When cutting hot peppers, disposable gloves are recommended. Avoid touching your face.

cordon bleu potato soup

Noelle Myers • Grand Forks, North Dakota
I came up with this recipe when I was looking for a way to use up some leftover ingredients. It's incredible! It's also an easy way to simmer up some hearty comfort in a hurry on chilly days.

2	cans (10-3/4 ounces *each*) condensed cream of potato soup, undiluted
1	can (14-1/2 ounces) chicken broth
1	cup (4 ounces) shredded Swiss cheese
1	cup diced fully cooked ham
1	cup whole milk
1	can (5 ounces) chunk white chicken, drained
2	teaspoons Dijon mustard

In a 2-qt. microwave-safe dish, combine all the ingredients. Cover and microwave on high for 5-8 minutes or until heated through, stirring twice. **yield: 4 servings.**

Editor's Note: This recipe was tested in a 1,100-watt microwave.

autumn chowder

Sheena Hoffman
North Vancouver, British Columbia
When the temperature begins to drop, we enjoy satisfying foods like this robust chowder. It's simple to prepare, and the aroma of it as it cooks makes my mouth water.

2	bacon strips, diced
1/4	cup chopped onion
1	medium red potato, cubed
1	small carrot, halved lengthwise and thinly sliced
1/2	cup water
3/4	teaspoon chicken bouillon granules
1	cup milk
2/3	cup frozen corn
1/8	teaspoon pepper
2-1/2	teaspoons all-purpose flour
2	tablespoons cold water
3/4	cup shredded cheddar cheese

In a large saucepan, cook bacon over medium heat until crisp; remove to paper towels. Drain, reserving 1 teaspoon drippings. In the drippings, saute onion until tender. Add the potato, carrot, water and bouillon. Bring to a boil. Reduce heat; cover and simmer for 15-20 minutes or until the vegetables are almost tender.

Stir in the milk, corn and pepper. Cook 5 minutes longer. Combine the flour and cold water until smooth; gradually whisk into soup. Bring to a boil; cook and stir for 1-2 minutes or until thickened. Remove from the heat; stir in cheese until melted. Sprinkle with bacon. **yield: 2 servings.**

autumn chowder

apricot turkey sandwiches

Charlotte Gehle • Brownstown, Michigan

Apricot jam adds a hint of sweetness to this savory sandwich that's piled high with fresh veggies.

- 2 turkey bacon strips
- 4 pieces multigrain bread, toasted
- 2 tablespoons apricot jam
- 3 ounces thinly sliced deli peppered turkey
- 2 slices tomato
- 2 slices red onion
- 2 pieces leaf lettuce
- 2 slices reduced-fat Swiss cheese
- 4 teaspoons Dijon mustard

In a small skillet, cook bacon over medium heat until crisp. Remove to paper towels to drain; set aside. Spread two toast slices with jam. Layer with the next five ingredients. Spread remaining toast with mustard; place on top. **yield: 2 servings.**

elegant mushroom soup

Marjorie Jaeger • Enderlin, North Dakota

This great recipe turns commonplace ingredients into a wonderfully delectable soup. My family is delighted whenever they know it's on the menu.

- 1 large onion, chopped
- 1/2 pound fresh mushrooms, sliced
- 2 tablespoons butter
- 2 tablespoons all-purpose flour
- 1/4 teaspoon pepper
- 1/8 teaspoon salt
- 1 cup milk
- 1 cup chicken broth
- 1 tablespoon minced fresh parsley

Ground nutmeg, optional

Sour cream

In a large saucepan, saute onion and mushrooms in butter for 3 minutes or until onion is tender. Stir in the flour, pepper and salt; gradually add milk and broth.

Bring to a boil; cook and stir for 2 minutes or until thickened. Add parsley and nutmeg if desired. Top individual servings with a dollop of sour cream. **yield: 2-3 servings.**

asian shrimp soup

asian shrimp soup

Michelle Smith • Sykesville, Maryland

I love this soup so much, I sometimes double the recipe. In fact, I've nicknamed it the "House Specialty!" If I have leftover chicken or pork on hand, I sometimes substitute it for the shrimp.

- 1 ounce uncooked thin spaghetti, broken into 1-inch pieces
- 3 cups plus 1 tablespoon water, *divided*
- 3 teaspoons reduced-sodium chicken bouillon granules
- 1/2 teaspoon salt
- 1/2 cup sliced fresh mushrooms
- 1/2 cup fresh *or* frozen corn
- 1 teaspoon cornstarch
- 1-1/2 teaspoons reduced-sodium teriyaki sauce
- 1 cup thinly sliced romaine lettuce
- 1 can (6 ounces) small shrimp, rinsed and drained
- 2 tablespoons sliced green onion

Cook pasta according to package directions. In a large saucepan, combine 3 cups water, bouillon and salt; bring to a boil. Stir in mushrooms and corn. Reduce heat; cook, uncovered, until vegetables are tender.

Combine the cornstarch, teriyaki sauce and remaining water until smooth; stir into soup. Bring to a boil; cook and stir for 1-2 minutes or until slightly thickened. Reduce heat. Drain pasta; add the pasta, lettuce, shrimp and green onion to the soup; heat through. **yield: 4 servings.**

sides, salads & breads

Round out your meal for two with this assortment of mouthwatering vegetable, rice and potato side dishes, plus refreshing salads. You'll find something for every entree and season.

fettuccine with green vegetables, page 63

cheesy onion biscuits

cooking tip

When it comes to selecting side dishes, the entree and side dish should complement one another. If your entree has intense flavor, pair it with more mild-flavored side dishes and vice versa. If your entree has lots of garlic, onion or nuts, stay away from a side dish that's loaded with any of those same ingredients.

Taste of Home Test Kitchen

Fresh from our home economists, these scone-shaped biscuits have a savory onion-and-cheddar flavor and a golden shell. Serve them with a pat of butter alongside your favorite soup or salad.

cheesy onion biscuits

1/4   **cup chopped onion**
3/4   **cup all-purpose flour**
1/8   **teaspoon baking powder**
1/8   **teaspoon baking soda**
1/8   **teaspoon salt**
  1   **tablespoon shortening**
1/4   **cup shredded cheddar cheese**
1/3   **cup buttermilk**

Place onion in a small microwave-safe bowl; cover and microwave on high for 1-2 minutes or until tender. In a small bowl, combine the flour, baking powder, baking soda and salt. Cut in shortening until mixture resembles coarse crumbs. Stir in cheese and onion. Stir in buttermilk just until moistened.

Turn onto a lightly floured surface; knead 8-10 times. Pat or roll out into a 4-in. circle; cut into four wedges. Place 2 in. apart on a baking sheet coated with cooking spray. Bake at 450° for 8-12 minutes or until golden brown. Serve warm. **yield: 4 biscuits.**

Editor's Note: This recipe was tested in a 1,100-watt microwave.

garlic-herb orzo pilaf

Mary Relyea • Canastota, New York

Mildly flavored and flecked with garlic and fresh herbs, this creamy, versatile pilaf can accompany a wide variety of entrees. Plus, it's a cinch to put together.

8	garlic cloves, peeled and thinly sliced
1	tablespoon olive oil
1/2	cup uncooked orzo pasta
1/2	cup uncooked long grain rice
1	can (14-1/2 ounces) reduced-sodium chicken broth *or* vegetable broth
1/3	cup water
3	green onions, thinly sliced
1/3	cup thinly sliced fresh basil leaves
1/4	cup minced fresh parsley
1/4	teaspoon salt

In a large nonstick skillet coated with cooking spray, cook garlic in oil over medium-high heat for 2 minutes. Add orzo and rice; cook 4-6 minutes longer or until lightly browned.

Stir in broth and water. Bring to a boil. Reduce heat; cover and simmer for 15-20 minutes or until rice is tender and liquid is absorbed. Stir in the onions, basil, parsley and salt. **yield: 4 servings.**

garlic-herb orzo pilaf

spaghetti squash supreme

spaghetti squash supreme

Jean Williams • Stillwater, Oklahoma

I often use the empty squash shells as serving platters for this unique side dish. The bacon complements the squash and Swiss cheese combination nicely. It's attractive and tasty!

1	large spaghetti squash (3-1/2 pounds)
4	bacon strips, diced
3	tablespoons butter
1	tablespoon brown sugar
1/2	teaspoon salt
1/4	teaspoon pepper
1/2	cup shredded Swiss cheese

Cut squash in half lengthwise; discard seeds. Place one squash half cut side down on a microwave-safe plate. Cover and microwave on high for 8 minutes or until easily pierced with a fork, turning once. Repeat with second squash half. When cool enough to handle, scoop out the squash, separating the strands with a fork; set squash aside.

In a large skillet, cook bacon over medium heat until crisp. Using a slotted spoon, remove to paper towels; drain, reserving drippings. Add the butter, brown sugar, salt and pepper to the drippings. Stir in squash and bacon; heat through. Remove from the heat; stir in the shredded Swiss cheese just until blended. Serve immediately. **yield: 4 servings.**

southern fried okra

Pam Duncan • Summers, Arkansas

Nothing beats a batch of okra, fresh from the garden. Golden brown, with a little green color showing through, these fried okra nuggets are crunchy and flavorful. My sons like to dip the pieces in ketchup.

1-1/2   cups sliced fresh *or* frozen okra, thawed
3   tablespoons buttermilk
2   tablespoons all-purpose flour
2   tablespoons cornmeal
1/4   teaspoon salt
1/4   teaspoon garlic herb seasoning blend
1/8   teaspoon pepper
Oil for frying
Additional salt and pepper, optional

Pat okra dry with paper towels. Place buttermilk in a shallow bowl. In another shallow bowl, combine the flour, cornmeal, salt, seasoning blend and pepper. Dip okra in buttermilk, then roll in cornmeal mixture.

In an electric skillet or deep-fat fryer, heat 1 in. of oil to 375°. Fry okra, a few pieces at a time, for 1-1/2 to 2-1/2 minutes on each side or until golden brown. Drain on paper towels. Season with additional salt and pepper if desired. **yield: 2 servings.**

southern fried okra

creamy baked corn

Nancy Collins • Clearfield, Pennsylvania

This is an old recipe handed down from my mother-in-law; it is an especially good accompaniment to roast beef. The corn is moist and velvety with a souffle-like topping.

1   can (8-3/4 ounces) cream-style corn
8   saltines, crushed
1   tablespoon butter, melted
1/8   teaspoon salt
1/8   teaspoon pepper
1   egg
1/4   cup 2% milk

In a small bowl, combine the corn, saltines, butter, salt and pepper. Transfer to a shallow 2-cup baking dish coated with cooking spray.

In a small bowl, whisk egg and milk; pour over corn mixture. Bake, uncovered, at 350° for 40-45 minutes or until a knife inserted near the center comes out clean. **yield: 2 servings.**

whole wheat biscuits

Edna Hoffman • Hebron, Indiana

I've had this recipe in my file for a long time. I love cooking and baking and am always creating something new. I thought the substitution of whole wheat flour gave these biscuits a deliciously different taste and texture.

1/3   cup all-purpose flour
1/3   cup whole wheat flour
1   tablespoon sugar
3/4   teaspoon baking powder
1/4   teaspoon baking soda
1/4   teaspoon salt
2   tablespoons cold butter
1/4   cup buttermilk

In a small bowl, combine the first six ingredients. Cut in butter until crumbly. Stir in the buttermilk just until ingredients are moistened.

Turn onto a floured surface; knead 6-8 times. Pat or roll out to 1-in. thickness; cut with a 2-1/2-in. biscuit cutter. Place biscuits on a greased baking sheet. Bake at 375° for 18-20 minutes or until lightly browned. **yield: 4 biscuits.**

buttery garlic potatoes

1/4   teaspoon ground cinnamon
3   tablespoons old-fashioned oats
1   cup plus 2 tablespoons bread flour
2-1/4   teaspoons bread machine yeast
3   tablespoons dried cranberries *or* raisins

In a small bread machine pan, place all ingredients in order suggested by manufacturer. Select basic bread setting. Bake according to bread machine directions (check dough after 5 minutes of mixing; add 1 to 2 teaspoons of water or flour if needed). **yield: 1 loaf (3/4 pound, 8 slices).**

Editor's Note: This recipe was tested in a West Bend brand Just for Dinner bread machine. This machine makes a 3/4-pound loaf. Recipe should not be doubled for use in a larger machine.

buttery garlic potatoes

Heidi Iacovetto • Phippsburg, Colorado
My husband and three boys all love oven-roasted potatoes. Unfortunately, busy weeknights usually don't leave me with time to prepare them. I whipped up this speedy and very tasty microwave recipe with red potatoes and seasonings instead, and everyone likes it.

6   small red potatoes, quartered
1/4   cup butter, melted
1   teaspoon seasoned salt
1   teaspoon paprika
1   teaspoon dried parsley flakes
1   teaspoon minced garlic

Place the potatoes in a 2-qt. microwave-safe dish. In a small bowl, combine the butter, seasoned salt, paprika, parsley and garlic; pour over potatoes and toss to coat.

Microwave, uncovered, on high for 8-10 minutes or until potatoes are tender, stirring frequently. **yield: 4 servings.**

Editor's Note: This recipe was tested in a 1,100-watt microwave.

cranberry oat bread

Dorothy Gilmore • Elburn, Illinois
In search of flavorful recipes for your small bread machine? Try this tender loaf. Cinnamon and tangy dried cranberries make it perfect for cold-weather mornings or afternoon tea.

1/2   cup water (80° to 90°)
1   tablespoon butter, softened
1   tablespoon honey
1/4   teaspoon salt

mandarin chicken coleslaw

Aileen Andreas Sox • Meridian, Idaho
With only five ingredients, this fast and fabulous supper salad is one recipe you'll want to keep handy all year long. Almonds add a delightful crunch to the fresh blend!

1-1/2   cups coleslaw mix
3/4   cup cubed cooked chicken breast
1   snack-size cup (4 ounces) mandarin oranges, drained
2   tablespoons chopped almonds
1/4   cup sesame ginger salad dressing

In a small bowl, combine the coleslaw, chicken, oranges and almonds. Drizzle with dressing and toss to coat; serve immediately. **yield: 2 servings.**

mandarin chicken coleslaw

spinach salad with curry dressing

spinach salad with curry dressing

Taste of Home Test Kitchen

This lively salad is packed with good-for-you fixings! Straight from our home economists, the spinach leaves and colorful fruits are topped with toasted pecans and a zippy homemade curry dressing.

- 3 cups fresh baby spinach
- 3/4 cup orange segments
- 1/2 small onion, thinly sliced
- 1/3 cup fresh blueberries
- 2 tablespoons chopped pecans, toasted

DRESSING:
- 1 tablespoon canola oil
- 1 tablespoon rice vinegar
- 1 tablespoon balsamic vinegar
- 2 teaspoons honey
- 1 teaspoon Dijon mustard
- 1/2 teaspoon curry powder

Dash salt

On two salad plates, arrange the spinach, orange segments, onion and blueberries. Sprinkle with pecans. In a small bowl, whisk the dressing ingredients. Drizzle over salads. **yield: 2 servings.**

tarragon corn on the cob

Brandy Jenkins • Greenwood, Mississippi
Nothing says summer like grilled corn. These ears, smothered in a tarragon butter, make summertime eating a real treat!

- 4 large ears sweet corn, husks removed
- 4 tarragon sprigs
- 1/3 cup butter, melted
- 4 teaspoons reduced-sodium soy sauce
- 2 teaspoons minced fresh tarragon *or* 1/2 teaspoon dried tarragon

Place each ear of corn with a tarragon sprig on a 14-in. x 12-in. piece of heavy-duty foil. Fold foil over corn and seal tightly. Grill corn, covered, over medium heat for 25-30 minutes or until tender, turning occasionally. In a small bowl, combine the butter, soy sauce and minced tarragon. Open foil carefully to allow steam to escape; brush the ears of corn with the tarragon butter mixture. **yield: 4 servings.**

quinoa pilaf

Sonya Fox • Peyton, Colorado
I created this recipe after sampling quinoa at a local restaurant. This quick-cooking recipe is a tasty alternative to rice pilaf.

- 1 medium onion, chopped
- 1 medium carrot, finely chopped
- 1 teaspoon olive oil
- 1 garlic clove, minced
- 1 can (14-1/2 ounces) reduced-sodium chicken broth *or* vegetable broth
- 1/4 cup water
- 1/4 teaspoon salt
- 1 cup quinoa, rinsed

In a small nonstick saucepan coated with cooking spray, cook onion and carrot in oil for 2-3 minutes or until crisp-tender. Add garlic; cook 1 minute longer. Stir in the broth, water and salt; bring to a boil. Stir in quinoa; return to a boil. Reduce heat; cover and simmer for 12-15 minutes or until liquid is absorbed. Remove from the heat; let stand for 5 minutes. Fluff with a fork. **yield: 4 servings.**

Editor's Note: If using vegetable broth, omit the salt. Look for quinoa in the cereal, rice or organic food aisle.

quinoa pilaf

gingered orange beets

Marion Tipton
Phoenix, Arizona
My husband was pleasantly
surprised when he tried this
new twist on beets. The
orange and ginger are a
surprising complement,
making this particular
vegetable a wonderful
addition to any
holiday table.

gingered orange beets

1-1/2   pounds whole fresh beets (about
      4 medium), trimmed and cleaned
   6   tablespoons olive oil, *divided*
1/4   teaspoon salt
1/4   teaspoon white pepper
   1   tablespoon rice vinegar
   1   tablespoon thawed orange juice
      concentrate
1-1/2   teaspoons grated orange peel,
      divided
1/2   teaspoon minced fresh
      gingerroot

   1   medium navel orange, peeled, sectioned and chopped
1/3   cup pecan halves, toasted

Brush beets with 4 tablespoons oil; sprinkle with salt and pepper. Wrap loosely in foil; place on a baking sheet. Bake at 425° for 70-75 minutes or until fork-tender. Cool slightly.

In a small bowl, whisk the rice vinegar, orange juice concentrate, 1 teaspoon orange peel, ginger and remaining oil; set aside.

Peel beets and cut into wedges; place in a serving bowl. Add the orange sections and pecans. Drizzle with orange sauce and toss to coat. Sprinkle with remaining orange peel. **yield: 4 servings.**

mini italian herb bread

Mary Schneider • Aurora, Colorado

I like to plan a large Italian meal around this delicious bread. I also take several loaves to our charity bake sale, which are always gone in a matter of minutes.

1/2	cup water (80° to 90°)
1	tablespoon canola oil
1-1/3	cups bread flour
1	tablespoon grated Parmesan cheese
2	teaspoons sugar
1	teaspoon dried minced onion
1	teaspoon dried parsley flakes
1/2	teaspoon dried basil
1/4	teaspoon salt
1/4	teaspoon garlic powder
2-1/4	teaspoons bread machine *or* quick-rise yeast

In a small bread machine pan, place all ingredients in order suggested by manufacturer. Select basic bread setting. Bake according to bread machine directions (check dough after 5 minutes of mixing; add 1 to 2 tablespoons of water or flour if needed). **yield: 1 loaf (3/4 pound).**

Editor's Note: This recipe was tested in a West Bend brand Just For Dinner bread machine. This bread machine makes a 3/4-pound loaf. The recipe should not be doubled for use in a larger machine.

mini italian herb bread

greek garden salad

greek garden salad

Weda Mosellie • Phillipsburg, New Jersey

My Italian-American mother and Syrian-American father merged their skills to create this delectable salad. I still grow most of the ingredients myself and serve this medley often.

3	cups torn romaine
1	plum tomato, sliced
1/2	cup julienned sweet red pepper
1/2	cup sliced seeded peeled cucumber
1/3	cup garbanzo beans *or* chickpeas, rinsed and drained
1/4	cup sliced fennel bulb
1/4	cup chopped celery
6	pitted ripe *or* Greek olives
1	green onion, thinly sliced

DRESSING:

2	tablespoons lemon juice
1	tablespoon olive oil
1	garlic clove, minced
1	teaspoon minced fresh cilantro
1	teaspoon water
1/2	teaspoon minced fresh mint *or* 1/8 teaspoon dried mint
1/2	teaspoon minced fresh oregano *or* 1/8 teaspoon dried oregano
1/2	teaspoon grated lemon peel

Dash *each* salt and pepper

1	tablespoon crumbled reduced-fat feta cheese

In a large serving bowl, combine the romaine, tomato, pepper, cucumber, chickpeas, fennel, celery, olives and green onion.

For dressing, in a small bowl, whisk the lemon juice, oil, garlic, cilantro, water, mint, oregano, lemon peel, salt and pepper. Pour over salad; toss to coat. Sprinkle with cheese. **yield: 4 servings.**

peachy sweet potatoes

peachy sweet potatoes

Josie Bochek • Sturgeon Bay, Wisconsin
The microwave makes this special side a cinch to prepare. Juicy slices of fresh peach and cinnamon-sugar turn ordinary sweet potatoes into a standout recipe.

- 4 medium sweet potatoes
- 1 medium peach, peeled and chopped
- 3 tablespoons butter
- 2 tablespoons cinnamon-sugar

Dash salt

- 3 tablespoons chopped pecans, toasted

Scrub and pierce potatoes; place on a microwave-safe plate. Microwave, uncovered, on high for 10-12 minutes or until tender, turning once.

Meanwhile, in a small saucepan, combine the peach, butter, cinnamon-sugar and salt; bring to a boil. Cook and stir for 2-3 minutes or until the peach is tender. Cut an "X" in the top of each potato; fluff pulp with a fork. Spoon peach mixture into each potato. Sprinkle with pecans. **yield: 4 servings.**

Editor's Note: This recipe was tested in a 1,100-watt microwave.

onion au gratin

Carol Slocum • Mechanicville, New York
Even if you're not an onion lover, you'll like this simple casserole. With just 10 minutes of prep, it's easy to whip up.

- 1 cup thinly sliced sweet onion
- 2/3 cup condensed broccoli cheese soup, undiluted

- 1 cup stuffing mix
- 1/2 cup water
- 1 tablespoon butter, melted

In a small bowl, combine onion and soup. Transfer to a 1-qt. baking dish coated with cooking spray. In a small bowl, combine the stuffing mix, water and butter. Let stand for 5 minutes. Spoon over onion.

Bake, uncovered, at 350° for 25-30 minutes or until onion is tender and stuffing is browned. **yield: 2 cups.**

sweet & savory breadsticks

Taste of Home Test Kitchen
These convenient breadsticks are a winner when it comes to ease of preparation and taste. And with just five ingredients that come together quickly, we're sure you'll love them!

- 1 tube (11-1/2 ounces) refrigerated corn bread twists
- 1/4 cup butter, melted
- 1/3 cup packed brown sugar
- 1/2 teaspoon garlic salt
- 1/4 teaspoon onion powder

Unroll and separate bread twists into 16 pieces. Place butter in a shallow bowl. Combine the brown sugar, garlic salt and onion powder in another shallow bowl. Roll bread pieces in butter, then in brown sugar mixture.

Twist two pieces together. Pinch ends to seal. Place on an ungreased baking sheet. Repeat. Bake at 375° for 12-14 minutes or until golden brown. Serve warm. **Yield: 4 servings.**

sweet & savory breadsticks

fettuccine with green vegetables

fettuccine with green vegetables

Susan McCartney • Onalaska, Wisconsin
I like to serve this rich pasta side with a variety of entrees. It even goes great with burgers and other picnic fare. I always get requests for the recipe!

4	ounces uncooked fettuccine
1/4	pound fresh asparagus, trimmed and cut into 1-inch pieces
1	medium zucchini, chopped
1	tablespoon canola oil
1	green onion, thinly sliced
1	garlic clove, minced
1/4	cup frozen peas, thawed
1/4	teaspoon salt
1/8	teaspoon pepper
1/4	cup shredded Romano cheese
2	tablespoons minced fresh parsley
4	teaspoons minced chives

Additional shredded Romano cheese, optional

Cook fettuccine according to package directions. Meanwhile, in a small saucepan, bring 1/2 in. of water to a boil. Add asparagus; cover and boil for 3 minutes. Drain and immediately place asparagus in ice water. Drain and pat dry.

In a large nonstick skillet, saute the zucchini in oil for 3 minutes. Add onion and garlic; saute 1 minute longer. Add the peas, salt, pepper and asparagus; saute until vegetables are crisp-tender.

Drain fettuccine; add to vegetable mixture. Stir in the cheese, parsley and chives. Garnish with additional cheese if desired. **yield: 4 servings.**

ginger currant scones

Shelia Parker • Reno, Nevada
I add loads of currants to the dough for flaky and attractive scones. Served warm with a drizzle of honey, these treats are a welcome addition to any meal.

1-1/2	cups all-purpose flour
1/3	cup sugar
1	teaspoon baking powder
1/2	teaspoon baking soda
6	tablespoons cold butter, cubed
1/2	cup buttermilk
3/4	cup dried currants
1/2	teaspoon minced fresh gingerroot
2	teaspoons honey

In a small bowl, combine the flour, sugar, baking powder and baking soda. Cut in butter until mixture resembles coarse crumbs. Add buttermilk just until moistened. Stir in currants and ginger. Turn onto a floured surface; knead 10 times.

Pat or roll out dough to 1-in. thickness; cut with a floured 2-1/2-in. biscuit cutter. Place 2 in. apart on a baking sheet coated with cooking spray.

Bake at 375° for 20-25 minutes or until golden brown. Drizzle with honey. Serve warm. **yield: 4 scones.**

ginger currant scones

chef's salad

Frank McReynolds • Carmichael, California
Red pepper flakes add bite to this fresh-tasting salad. It's extraordinarily tasty and delightful for any season.

- 3 cups spring mix salad greens
- 2 slices deli ham (1 ounce *each*), julienned
- 2 slices deli turkey (1 ounce *each*), julienned
- 1 medium tomato, chopped
- 1/2 cup julienned sweet yellow pepper
- 1/2 cup cubed cheddar cheese
- 1/4 cup chopped red onion
- 3 tablespoons chopped walnuts
- 2 tablespoons dried cranberries
- 2 tablespoons sliced ripe olives
- 1/2 teaspoon Beau Monde seasoning
- 1/4 to 1/2 teaspoon coarsely ground pepper
- 1/4 teaspoon crushed red pepper flakes

Salad dressing of your choice

In a large bowl, combine the first 13 ingredients. Serve with salad dressing of your choice. **yield: 2 servings.**

buttery sour cream muffins

Mary Cleckley • Slaton, Texas
This quick recipe is ideal when you're in a hurry. It's great with soup or beef stew. These moist muffins are filled with buttery flavor. Try serving them with fresh fruit.

- 1/2 cup self-rising flour
- 1/4 cup butter, melted
- 1/4 cup sour cream
- 1 tablespoon water

In a small bowl, combine the flour, butter, sour cream and water. Coat muffin cups with cooking spray; fill three-fourths full.

Bake at 350° for 18-20 minutes or until a toothpick inserted near the center comes out clean. Cool for 5 minutes before removing from pan to a wire rack. Serve warm. **yield: 3 servings.**

Editor's Note: As a substitute for self-rising flour, place 3/4 teaspoon baking powder and 1/4 teaspoon salt in a 1/2 cup measuring cup. Add all-purpose flour to measure 1/2 cup.

twice-baked deviled potatoes

twice-baked deviled potatoes

Karol Chandler-Ezell • Nacogdoches, Texas
These irresistible spuds are flavored with bacon and cheddar and have just a hint of Dijon mustard. Since they take under 30 minutes to make, they're perfect for weeknight dinners.

- 4 small baking potatoes
- 1/4 cup butter, softened
- 1/4 cup milk
- 1 cup (4 ounces) shredded cheddar cheese
- 1/3 cup real bacon bits
- 2 green onions, chopped
- 1 teaspoon Dijon mustard

Dash paprika

Scrub and pierce potatoes; place on a microwave-safe plate. Microwave, uncovered, on high for 7-10 minutes or until tender, turning once. Let stand for 5 minutes. Cut a thin slice off the top of each potato and discard. Scoop out pulp, leaving a thin shell.

In a large bowl, mash the pulp with butter and milk. Stir in the cheese, bacon, onions, mustard and paprika. Spoon into potato shells. Return to the microwave-safe plate. Microwave, uncovered, on high for 1-2 minutes or until cheese is melted. **yield: 4 servings.**

Editor's Note: This recipe was tested in a 1,100-watt microwave.

Blaine Baker
Kelseyville, California
I use carrots dug fresh from our garden to make this colorful casserole. Its creamy, buttery texture makes folks "root" for this comforting side dish.

carrot casserole

4	**medium carrots, sliced**
1/3	**cup finely chopped green pepper**
1	**tablespoon finely chopped onion**
2	**tablespoons plus 2 teaspoons butter,** *divided*
4	**teaspoons all-purpose flour**
1/4	**teaspoon salt**
1/8	**teaspoon pepper**
1	**can (5-1/2 ounces) evaporated milk**
1	**teaspoon minced jalapeno pepper, optional**
1	**teaspoon dried parsley flakes**
1/4	**teaspoon dried savory**
2	**tablespoons dry bread crumbs**

Place 1 in. of water in a small saucepan; add carrots. Bring to a boil. Reduce heat; cover and simmer for 7-9 minutes or until crisp-tender. Drain and set aside.

In a small skillet, saute green pepper and onion in 2 tablespoons butter until tender. Stir in the flour, salt and pepper until smooth. Gradually add the evaporated milk. Bring to a boil; cook and stir for 2 minutes or until thickened.

Stir in jalapeno if desired, parsley, savory and carrots. Transfer to a 2-cup baking dish coated with cooking spray.

In a small skillet, melt remaining butter. Add bread crumbs; cook and stir until toasted and browned. Sprinkle over casserole. Bake, uncovered, at 350° for 15-20 minutes or until bubbly. **yield: 3 servings.**

Editor's Note: When cutting hot peppers, disposable gloves are recommended. Avoid touching your face.

dilled fall vegetables

dilled fall vegetables

Janice Mitchell • Aurora, Colorado
Dish up a healthy serving of root vegetables seasoned with dill in this colorful, easy-to-fix combo. I sometimes substitute celery for the turnips, and always get compliments.

- 1 cup sliced carrots
- 1 cup chopped peeled turnips
- 2 tablespoons lemon juice
- 1 tablespoon canola oil
- 1 tablespoon honey
- 1/4 teaspoon dill weed
Salt and pepper to taste

Place 1 in. of water in a saucepan; add carrots and turnips. Bring to a boil. Reduce heat; cover and simmer for 7-9 minutes or until crisp-tender. Drain. Combine the remaining ingredients; drizzle over vegetables and toss lightly. **yield: 2 servings.**

honey oatmeal bread

Marilyn Smith • Green Bay, Wisconsin
Of all the breads I make, this is my husband's favorite. The subtle honey and oat flavor makes it perfect for toast or sandwiches...or as a side with a hot bowl of soup.

- 1/2 cup water (80° to 90°)
- 1 tablespoon canola oil
- 4 teaspoons honey
- 1/4 teaspoon salt
- 1/4 cup quick-cooking oats
- 1-1/4 cups bread flour
- 2-1/4 teaspoons bread machine *or* quick-rise yeast

In a small bread machine pan, place all ingredients in order suggested by manufacturer. Select basic bread setting. Bake according to bread machine directions (check dough after 5 minutes of mixing; add 1 to 2 tablespoons of water or flour if needed). **yield: 1 loaf (3/4 pound, 8 slices).**

Editor's Note: This recipe was tested in a West Bend brand Just for Dinner bread machine. This machine makes a 3/4-pound loaf. Recipe should not be doubled for use in a larger machine.

hearty baked beans

Taste of Home Test Kitchen
Old-fashioned baked beans get jazzed up with garlic, brown sugar and mustard in this downsized version created by our home economists.

- 1 small onion, chopped
- 1 bacon strip, chopped
- 1/4 teaspoon minced garlic
- 1 can (8 ounces) pork and beans
- 3/4 cup canned kidney beans, rinsed and drained
- 2 tablespoons brown sugar
- 1 tablespoon cider vinegar
- 1/8 teaspoon ground mustard

In a small skillet, saute onion and bacon until onion is tender; drain. Add minced garlic; cook 1 minute longer. Stir in the pork and beans, kidney beans, brown sugar, cider vinegar and ground mustard. Cook, uncovered, for 5 minutes, stirring occasionally.

Transfer to a 2-cup baking dish coated with cooking spray. Cover and bake at 350° for 25-30 minutes or until bubbly. **yield: 2 servings.**

hearty baked beans

sweet potato fries

sweet potato fries

Kelly McWherter • Houston, Texas
Nutritious sweet potatoes give these extra-crunchy fries a tasty twist. With the yummy mayo-chutney dip, this super side could double as a party appetizer!

- 2 tablespoons beaten egg
- 1 tablespoon water
- 1/3 cup dry bread crumbs
- 2 tablespoons grated Parmesan cheese
- 1/4 teaspoon cayenne pepper
- 1/4 teaspoon pepper
- 1 large sweet potato (14 ounces), peeled
- 2 teaspoons olive oil

MANGO CHUTNEY MAYONNAISE:
- 1/4 cup mayonnaise
- 2 tablespoons mango chutney
- 1/4 teaspoon curry powder

Dash salt
- 2 teaspoons minced fresh parsley, optional

In a shallow bowl, whisk egg and water. In a resealable plastic bag, combine the bread crumbs, cheese, cayenne and pepper. Cut sweet potato into 1/4-in. strips. Add to egg mixture, a few at a time, and toss to coat. Add to the crumb mixture, a few at a time; seal bag and shake to coat.

Arrange potato strips in a single layer on a baking sheet coated with cooking spray; drizzle with oil. Bake at 450° for 25-30 minutes or until golden brown and crisp, turning occasionally.

In a small bowl, combine the mayonnaise, chutney, curry powder and salt. If desired, sprinkle minced fresh parsley over fries. Serve sweet potato fries with mango chutney mayonnaise. **yield: 2 servings.**

walnut rice

Vera Whisner • Elkton, Maryland
I get rave reviews whenever I serve this, and there are never any leftovers. The short prep and cooking times are an added bonus to its mouthwatering taste.

- 2/3 cup chopped walnuts
- 1/3 cup chopped onion
- 1 tablespoon sesame seeds
- 1/4 teaspoon salt
- 1/4 teaspoon garlic powder
- 3 tablespoons butter
- 1-1/2 cups hot water
- 2 tablespoons soy sauce
- 1-1/2 cups frozen broccoli florets
- 1 cup uncooked instant rice

In a large skillet, saute the walnuts, onion, sesame seeds, salt and garlic powder in butter until onion is tender and sesame seeds are golden brown. Add water and soy sauce; bring to a boil. Stir in broccoli and rice. Cover and remove from the heat. Let stand for 5 minutes or until rice is tender. **yield: 4 servings.**

tangy baked beans

Dean Copeland • Ochlocknee, Georgia
Different, delicious and sized exactly right for two people, this simple, breezy, home-style side dish is sure to please!

- 2 bacon strips, cut into 1-inch pieces
- 2 tablespoons strong brewed coffee
- 4 teaspoons brown sugar
- 1 teaspoon cider vinegar
- 1/4 teaspoon ground mustard
- 1/8 teaspoon salt
- 1 can (8.3 ounces) baked beans, undrained
- 1/2 cup chopped onion

In a small skillet, cook bacon over medium heat until partially cooked but not crisp. Meanwhile, in a small saucepan, combine the coffee, brown sugar, vinegar, mustard and salt. Bring to a boil; cook and stir for 2-3 minutes or until the sugar is dissolved. Stir in the beans and chopped onion.

Drain bacon on paper towels. Divide the bean mixture between two 6-oz. ramekins or custard cups coated with cooking spray. Top with bacon. Bake at 350° for 25-30 minutes or until bubbly. **yield: 2 servings.**

acorn squash with cranberry stuffing

Dorothy Pritchett • Wills Point, Texas

You just can't go wrong with this recipe if you have squash or cranberry lovers at your table. The blend of flavors is delectable and colorful and goes great with a traditional holiday dinner.

2	medium acorn squash
1/4	cup chopped celery
2	tablespoons chopped onion
2	tablespoons butter
1	medium tart apple, peeled and diced
1/2	teaspoon salt
1/2	teaspoon lemon juice
1/8	teaspoon pepper
1	cup fresh *or* frozen cranberries
1/2	cup sugar
2	tablespoons water

Cut squash in half; discard seeds. Cut a thin slice from the bottom of squash halves so they sit flat. Place squash hollow side down in an ungreased 13-in. x 9-in. baking dish. Add 1/2 in. of water. Cover and bake at 375° for 45 minutes.

Meanwhile, in a small skillet, saute celery and onion in butter until tender. Add the apple, salt, lemon juice and pepper. Cook, uncovered, over medium-low heat until apple is tender, stirring occasionally. Stir in the cranberries, sugar and water. Cook and stir until berries pop and liquid is syrupy.

Turn squash halves over; fill with cranberry mixture. Cover and bake 10-15 minutes longer or until squash is tender. **yield: 4 servings.**

cheddar basil cauliflower

acorn squash with cranberry stuffing

cheddar basil cauliflower

David Harper • Clackamas, Oregon

Fresh basil adds a unique burst of Italian flair to this classic side dish. Perfect for chillier days, this comforting recipe is sure to warm you up!

2-1/2	cups small fresh cauliflowerets
1	tablespoon white wine *or* water
1-1/2	teaspoons minced fresh basil *or* 1/2 teaspoon dried basil
1	teaspoon water
1	teaspoon canola oil
1/2	teaspoon sugar
1/4	teaspoon salt
1/3	cup shredded cheddar cheese

In a small saucepan, combine the first seven ingredients. Cover and cook over medium heat for 10-12 minutes or until cauliflower is tender, stirring once. Transfer to a small serving bowl; sprinkle with cheese. **yield: 2 servings.**

blt bread salad

Tonya Vowels • Vine Grove, Kentucky
Zesty and fun, this salad always draws a positive response. It tastes just like a BLT, has a light vinaigrette dressing and is fabulous with many main dishes—or alone!

- 3 cups cubed French bread
- 1 tablespoon water
- 1 tablespoon white wine vinegar
- 1 tablespoon reduced-fat mayonnaise
- 1-1/4 teaspoons sugar
- 1 teaspoon olive oil
- 1-1/2 cups torn leaf lettuce
- 1 large tomato, chopped
- 2 tablespoons crumbled cooked bacon
- 1 tablespoon chopped green onion

Place the bread cubes on an ungreased baking sheet. Coat the baking sheet lightly with cooking spray. Bake at 400° for 8-10 minutes or until bread cubes are toasted and golden brown.

For dressing, in a small bowl, whisk the water, white wine vinegar, mayonnaise, sugar and olive oil until smooth. In a large salad bowl, combine the lettuce, chopped tomato and toasted bread cubes.

blt bread salad

Sprinkle the salad with the crumbled bacon and chopped green onion. Drizzle with dressing and toss to coat. **yield: 4 servings.**

cilantro corn saute

Lisa Langston • Conroe, Texas
This is an easy accompaniment with most anything. With cilantro and cumin, it's strong on Southwest flavor.

- 3-1/3 cups fresh *or* frozen corn, thawed
- 1 medium green pepper, chopped
- 1 tablespoon finely chopped onion
- 2 tablespoons butter
- 1/2 cup minced fresh cilantro
- 1-1/2 teaspoons ground cumin

In a large skillet, saute the corn, green pepper and onion in butter until tender. Stir in cilantro and cumin; saute 1-2 minutes longer or until heated through. **yield: 4 servings.**

pistachio cranberry orzo

Barbara Spitzer • Lodi, California
This recipe was originally an entree with chicken and linguini. I keep changing the ingredients to go with whatever else I'm serving for dinner, but my husband prefers this version.

- 1/3 cup uncooked orzo pasta
- 1 shallot, finely chopped
- 2 teaspoons olive oil
- 2 teaspoons butter
- 1/4 cup pistachios, chopped
- 1/4 cup dried cranberries
- 1/4 cup heavy whipping cream
- 1/4 cup chicken broth
- 3 tablespoons marsala wine *or* additional chicken broth

Dash salt and pepper

Cook orzo according to package directions. Meanwhile, in a nonstick skillet, saute shallot in oil and butter for 1 minute. Add the pistachios; saute for 1-2 minutes or until lightly browned.

Stir in the cranberries, cream, broth and wine or additional broth. Cook mixture over medium heat for 3-4 minutes or until thickened. Drain the orzo; add to the cranberry mixture. Season orzo with salt and pepper. **yield: 2 servings.**

cooking tip

2

Serving a side dish with your meal should add more flavor...not more work! For easy of preparation, look for oven-baked side dishes that cook at the same temperature as your oven entree. Or for a refreshing break from the hot foods, make a tossed salad, an assortment of fresh fruit or a tried-and-true relish tray. Make-ahead recipes also keep things simple.

Claudia Ruiss
Massapequa,
New York

This fluffy and flavorful couscous takes only moments to prepare. I use couscous a lot because it cooks quickly and is so versatile—you can add almost any vegetable to it.

couscous with mushrooms

1-1/4 **cups water**
2 **tablespoons butter**
2 **teaspoons chicken bouillon granules**
1/4 **teaspoon salt**
1/4 **teaspoon pepper**

1 **cup uncooked couscous**
1 **can (7 ounces) mushroom stems and pieces, drained**

In a large saucepan, bring the water, butter, bouillon, salt and pepper to a boil. Stir in couscous and mushrooms. Cover and remove from the heat; let stand for 5 minutes. Fluff with a fork. **yield: 4 servings.**

calico corn cakes

Taste of Home Test Kitchen

Served with salsa on the side, these fluffy corn cakes from our home ecomonists make a fantastic side for nearly any main dish, especially those with Southwestern flair. Try serving them with sour cream on the side for a little extra kick.

- 1/4   cup chopped onion
- 1/4   cup chopped green pepper
- 1   teaspoon canola oil
- 1/4   cup all-purpose flour
- 2   tablespoons yellow cornmeal
- 1/2   teaspoon sugar
- 1/4   teaspoon salt
- 1/4   teaspoon dried oregano
- 1/8   teaspoon baking powder
- 1/8   teaspoon ground cumin
- 1   egg, lightly beaten
- 1/4   cup 2% milk
- 1   cup frozen corn, thawed
- 1   tablespoon diced pimientos
- 1/2   cup salsa

In a small skillet, saute onion and green pepper in oil until tender; set aside. In a large bowl, whisk the flour, cornmeal, sugar, salt, oregano, baking powder, cumin, egg and milk just until combined. Fold in the corn, pimientos and onion mixture.

Heat a large skillet coated with cooking spray; drop batter by 1/4 cupfuls into skillet. Cook for 3 minutes on each side or until golden brown. Serve cakes with salsa. **yield: 3 servings.**

calico corn cakes

cranberry scones

Della Dunsieth • New Castle, Pennsylvania

You can use any dried fruit for these tender scones, but my favorite is a mix of dried cranberries and golden raisins. The sweetness of these delightful baked treats is a nice contrast to the usual savory sides.

- 1   cup all-purpose flour
- 1/4   cup sugar
- 1-1/2   teaspoons baking powder
- 1/8   teaspoon salt
- 1/4   cup cold butter
- 3   tablespoons 2% milk
- 1   egg, beaten
- 1/4   cup dried cranberries
- 1/4   teaspoon coarse sugar

In a small bowl, combine the flour, sugar, baking powder and salt. Cut in butter until mixture resembles coarse crumbs. In a small bowl, combine milk and 2 tablespoons beaten egg; add to crumb mixture just until moistened. Stir in cranberries.

Turn onto a floured surface; knead gently 6-8 times. Pat into a 6-in. circle. Cut dough into four wedges. Separate the wedges and place on a baking sheet coated with cooking spray. Brush scones with remaining egg; sprinkle with coarse sugar.

Bake at 425° for 12-15 minutes or until golden brown. Serve warm. **yield: 4 scones.**

main dishes

The perfect portion for two is easy thanks to these trimmed-back entrees. From pleasing poultry to succulent steak, seafood and more, deciding what's for dinner couldn't be easier.

apricot chicken pasta, page 87

cooking tip

To prepare asparagus, rinse stalks well in cold water. Snap off the stalk ends as far down as they will easily break when gently bent, or cut off the tough white portion. If stalks are large, use a vegetable peeler to gently peel the tough area of the stalk from the end to just below the tip. If tips are large, scrape off scales with a knife.

Cindy Dorsett
Lubbock, Texas

By using fantastic ingredients such as beef tenderloin, crabmeat and fresh asparagus, I created this elegant meal. Steak Oscar is a fine recipe combining the delicious taste of asparagus with only the finest of steaks around.

asparagus steak oscar

1 **envelope bearnaise sauce**
1 **pound fresh asparagus, trimmed**
1/4 **pound fresh crabmeat**
2 **tablespoons butter**
1/2 **teaspoon minced garlic**
1 **tablespoon lemon juice**
4 **beef tenderloin steaks (1 inch thick and 3 ounces *each*)**
1/8 **teaspoon paprika**

Prepare bearnaise sauce according to package directions. Meanwhile, place asparagus in a steamer basket; place in a large saucepan over 1 in. of water. Bring to a boil; cover and steam for 8-10 minutes or until crisp-tender.

In a large skillet, saute crab in butter for 3-4 minutes or until heated through. Add garlic; cook 1 minute longer. Stir in lemon juice; keep the sauce warm.

Grill steaks, covered, over medium heat or broil 4 in. from the heat for 6-8 minutes on each side or until meat reaches desired doneness (for medium-rare, a meat thermometer should read 145°; medium, 160°; well-done, 170°). Top with crab mixture, asparagus and bearnaise sauce. Sprinkle with paprika. **yield: 4 servings.**

herb-crusted red snapper

Nella Parker • Hersey, Michigan

An appetizing blend of herbs complements the mild flavor of these golden fillets. Red pepper flakes give the entree its zip.

1	tablespoon dry bread crumbs
1	teaspoon dried basil
1	teaspoon paprika
1/2	teaspoon salt
1/2	teaspoon fennel seeds
1/2	teaspoon dried thyme
1/2	teaspoon dried oregano
1/4	teaspoon pepper
1/4	teaspoon crushed red pepper flakes
2	red snapper fillets (5 ounces *each*), skin removed
2	teaspoons canola oil

In a food processor, combine the first nine ingredients; cover and process until fennel is finely ground. Transfer to a shallow bowl; dip fillets in herb mixture, coating both sides.

In a heavy skillet over medium-high heat, cook fillets in oil for 3-4 minutes on each side or until fish flakes easily with a fork. **yield: 2 servings.**

herb-crusted red snapper

pork with apples 'n' hazelnuts

pork with apples 'n' hazelnuts

Lorraine Caland • Thunder Bay, Ontario

When pork tenderloin is on sale, I buy several with this recipe in mind. Round out the meal with rolls and a green salad.

1	pork tenderloin (1 pound), cut into 1/4-inch slices
1	tablespoon olive oil
1	small onion, chopped
1	medium apple, cut into wedges
1	medium carrot, julienned
1/2	cup chicken broth
1	cup heavy whipping cream
2	tablespoons red wine vinegar
2	tablespoons Dijon mustard
1	tablespoon tomato paste

Dash salt and pepper

2	tablespoons chopped hazelnuts

In a large skillet, cook pork in oil over medium heat for 2-3 minutes on each side or until juices run clear. Remove and keep warm.

In the same pan, saute the onion, apple and carrot for 1 minute. Add broth; cook and stir for 5 minutes or until liquid is evaporated.

Stir in the cream, vinegar, mustard, tomato paste, salt and pepper. Bring to a boil. Reduce heat; simmer, uncovered, for 3-5 minutes or until sauce is slightly thickened. Return pork to the pan; stir to coat. Sprinkle with hazelnuts. **yield: 3-4 servings.**

glazed beef tournedos

Janet Singleton • Bellevue, Ohio

I found this wonderful, quick recipe in a book years ago. It's been a favorite for special occasions ever since! I like to serve it with twice-baked potatoes and a simple spinach salad.

- 3 **tablespoons steak sauce**
- 2 **tablespoons ketchup**
- 2 **tablespoons orange marmalade**
- 1 **tablespoon lemon juice**
- 1 **tablespoon finely chopped onion**
- 1 **garlic clove, minced**
- 4 **beef tenderloin steaks (6 ounces *each*)**

In a small bowl, combine the steak sauce, ketchup, marmalade, lemon juice, onion and garlic. Set aside 1/4 cup for serving.

Using long-handled tongs, moisten a paper towel with cooking oil and lightly coat the grill rack. Grill steaks, uncovered, over medium heat or broil 4 in. from heat for 5-7 minutes on each side or until meat reaches desired doneness (for medium-rare, a meat thermometer should read 145°; medium, 160°; well-done, 170°), basting frequently with remaining sauce.

Just before serving, brush steaks with reserved sauce.
yield: 4 servings.

glazed beef tournedos

cacciatore chicken breasts

cacciatore chicken breasts

JoAnn McCauley • Dubuque, Iowa

This easy recipe is my version of the traditional Italian specialty. The tasty sauce and chicken can be served over noodles or rice. If you want to lower the sodium, use garlic powder instead of garlic salt.

- 1/2 **medium onion, sliced and separated into rings**
- 1/2 **medium green pepper, sliced**
- 1 **tablespoon olive oil**
- 2 **boneless skinless chicken breast halves (5 ounces *each*)**
- 3/4 **cup canned stewed tomatoes**
- 2 **tablespoons white wine *or* chicken broth**
- 1/4 **teaspoon garlic salt**
- 1/4 **teaspoon dried rosemary, crushed**
- 1/8 **teaspoon pepper**

In a large skillet, saute onion and green pepper in oil until crisp-tender. Remove and keep warm. Cook chicken over medium-high heat for 4-5 minutes on each side or until juices run clear. Remove and keep warm.

Add the tomatoes, wine, garlic salt, rosemary and pepper to the skillet; cook and stir until heated through. Add the onion mixture. Serve the sauce with chicken.
yield: 2 servings.

pine nut-crusted tilapia

pine nut-crusted tilapia

Taste of Home Test Kitchen

This golden-brown fish has a tender texture, nutty coating and hint of sweet honey. It's fast to fix and can be served for a special family meal or when you want to impress guests.

- 1/2 cup pine nuts, ground
- 1/4 cup all-purpose flour
- 1/4 teaspoon dill weed
- 1/4 teaspoon lemon-pepper seasoning
- 1 egg
- 3 tablespoons lemon juice
- 1 teaspoon honey
- 4 tilapia fillets (6 ounces *each*)
- 2 tablespoons butter

Additional honey, optional

In a shallow bowl, combine the pine nuts, flour, dill and lemon-pepper. In another shallow bowl, combine the egg, lemon juice and honey. Dip fillets in egg mixture, then coat with nut mixture.

In a large nonstick skillet, cook fillets in butter over medium heat for 4-5 minutes on each side or until fish flakes easily with a fork. Drizzle with additional honey if desired. **yield: 4 servings.**

thai shrimp linguine

Paula Marchesi • Lenhartsville, Pennsylvania

My group always says "yum" when I serve this pasta pleaser. With a squeeze of lime juice and a few sprigs of cilantro, it's full of flavor.

- 1 package (9 ounces) refrigerated linguine
- 1 cup fresh snow peas
- 2 cups shredded carrots
- 1/2 pound sliced fresh mushrooms
- 1 tablespoon olive oil

- 1/2 pound uncooked medium shrimp, peeled and deveined
- 1 cup Thai peanut sauce

Cook linguine according to package directions, adding snow peas and linguine at the same time.

Meanwhile, in a large skillet, cook the carrots and mushrooms in oil over medium heat for 3 minutes. Add shrimp; cook and stir 3 minutes longer or until shrimp turn pink. Stir in peanut sauce; heat through.

Drain linguine and snow peas; transfer to a serving bowl. Top linguine and snowpeas with shrimp mixture; toss to coat. **yield: 3 servings.**

quick chicken cordon bleu

Louise Gilbert • Quesnel, British Columbia

I reworked this classic into a time-saving microwave dish. If you like, use cheddar cheese in place of Swiss.

- 4 boneless skinless chicken breast halves (6 ounces *each*)
- 4 thin slices deli ham
- 2 slices Swiss cheese, halved
- 1/4 cup butter, melted
- 1 envelope seasoned coating mix

Flatten chicken to 1/4-in. thickness. Place ham and cheese down the center of each; roll up and secure with a toothpick. Place butter and coating mix in separate shallow bowls. Dip the chicken in the butter, then roll in the coating mix.

Place in a greased 2-qt. microwave-safe dish. Cover loosely and microwave on high for 5-7 minutes on each side or until no longer pink. Let stand for 5 minutes. Discard toothpicks. **yield: 4 servings.**

Editor's Note: *This recipe was tested in a 1,100-watt microwave.*

quick chicken cordon bleu

seafood fettuccine alfredo

seafood fettuccine alfredo

Jimmy Spellings • Oakland, Tennessee
I like to serve this lovely main dish, featuring scallops and shrimp, with a loaf of freshly baked bread. Sprinkled with tomato and parsley, this entree looks simply tempting.

- 4 ounces uncooked fettuccine
- 1/4 pound uncooked medium shrimp, peeled and deveined
- 1/4 pound sea scallops, halved
- 2 tablespoons olive oil, *divided*
- 1 small shallot, chopped
- 1 garlic clove, minced
- 1/4 cup chicken broth
- 1/4 cup white wine *or additional chicken broth*
- 1 cup heavy whipping cream *or half-and-half cream*
- 1/2 cup grated Parmesan cheese
- 1 Roma tomato, diced
- 2 tablespoons minced fresh parsley

Cook the fettuccine according to package directions. Meanwhile, in a large skillet, saute shrimp and scallops in 1 tablespoon oil for 3-5 minutes or until shrimp turn pink and scallops are opaque. Remove and keep warm.

In the same skillet, saute shallot in remaining oil until tender. Add garlic; cook 1 minute longer. Stir in broth and wine. Bring to a boil. Reduce heat; simmer, uncovered, for 6-8 minutes or until most of the liquid has evaporated. Stir in cream; cook, uncovered, over medium heat for 5 minutes or until thickened.

Drain fettuccine; stir into cream sauce. Add shrimp, scallops and cheese; toss to coat. Sprinkle with tomato and parsley. **yield: 2 servings.**

mushroom-stuffed chicken breasts

Edie DeSpain • Logan, Utah
Stuffing mix, creates a crispy and mouthwatering coating for the chicken, as well as a tasty, moist filling.

- 1-1/2 cups chopped fresh mushrooms
- 1/4 cup chopped celery
- 1/4 cup chopped green onions
- 1/4 teaspoon dried marjoram
- 1/4 cup butter, *divided*
- 1 package (6 ounces) chicken-flavored stuffing mix, coarsely crushed, *divided*
- 4 boneless skinless chicken breast halves (6 ounces *each*)
- 1 egg
- 2 tablespoons milk
- 1 teaspoon paprika

In a small skillet, saute the mushrooms, celery, onions and marjoram in 2 tablespoons butter for 3-4 minutes or until vegetables are tender. Stir in 1/2 cup chicken-flavored stuffing mix.

Flatten chicken to 1/4-in. thickness. Spoon mushroom mixture down the center of each. Roll up and secure with toothpicks.

In a shallow bowl, whisk egg and milk. Place the remaining stuffing mix in another bowl; stir in paprika. Dip chicken in egg mixture, then coat with crumb mixture. Place seam side down in a greased 8-in. square baking dish.

Melt remaining butter; drizzle over chicken. Bake, uncovered, at 375° for 30-35 minutes or until meat is no longer pink. Discard toothpicks. **yield: 4 servings.**

mushroom-stuffed chicken breasts

John Slivon
Navarre Beach,
Florida
These individual potpies offer comforting flavor in every bite. Cut through the flaky, golden homemade crust to a rich, creamy broth brimming with hearty vegetables and juicy chunks of chicken.

individual chicken potpies

1	cup plus 2 tablespoons all-purpose flour, *divided*
1/4	teaspoon baking powder
1/4	teaspoon salt
3	tablespoons cold butter, *divided*
2	tablespoons buttermilk
1	tablespoon canola oil
1	to 2 tablespoons cold water
4	medium carrots, sliced
3	celery ribs, sliced
1	large onion, chopped
2-1/2	cups reduced-sodium chicken broth
2/3	cup fat-free milk
2	cups cubed cooked chicken breast
1	cup frozen peas
1/8	teaspoon pepper
1	egg white

Combine 3/4 cup flour, baking powder and salt. Cut in 2 tablespoons butter until crumbly. Add buttermilk and oil; toss with a fork. Gradually add water, tossing with a fork until dough forms a ball. Cover and refrigerate for 1 hour.

For filling, in a large skillet, melt remaining butter. Add the carrots, celery and onion; saute until crisp-tender. In a small bowl, combine remaining flour with the broth and milk until smooth. Gradually stir into vegetable mixture. Bring to a boil; cook and stir for 2 minutes or until thickened. Stir in the chicken, peas and pepper. Transfer to four 16-oz. ramekins; set aside.

Divide dough into four portions. On a lightly floured surface, roll out dough to fit ramekins. Place dough over chicken mixture; trim and seal edges. Cut out a decorative center or cut slits in pastry. Brush with the egg white.

Place ramekins on a baking sheet. Bake at 425° for 20-25 minutes or until crusts are golden brown. **yield: 4 servings.**

beef burgundy stew

Blanche Rattigan • Glen Burnie, Maryland

I was drawn to this recipe because it was a preparation for two. There was no special occasion to serve this dish, but I made it often because my mother, who was an excellent cook, loved it.

- 1/4 cup all-purpose flour
- 1/4 teaspoon salt
- 1/4 teaspoon pepper
- 3/4 pound beef top sirloin steak, cut into thin strips
- 2 tablespoons canola oil, *divided*
- 1 medium onion, thinly sliced
- 1 garlic clove, minced
- 2/3 cup beef broth
- 2/3 cup burgundy wine *or* additional beef broth
- 1/2 teaspoon dried basil
- Hot cooked egg noodles

In a large resealable plastic bag, combine the flour, salt and pepper; add beef, a few pieces at a time, and shake to coat.

In a small skillet, brown beef in 1 tablespoon oil on all sides; remove and set aside. In the same skillet, saute onion and garlic in remaining oil until tender.

Return beef to the pan; stir in the broth, wine and basil. Bring to a boil. Reduce heat; cover and simmer for 25-30 minutes or until meat is tender. Serve with egg noodles. **yield: 2 servings.**

beef burgundy stew

shrimp in herbs

Iola Egle • Bella Vista, Arkansas

Dressed up with two types of parsley and other garden-fresh herbs, this luscious and simply scrumptious shrimp entree makes any weeknight meal unique. You'll be surprised how quickly it comes together.

- 2 pounds uncooked medium shrimp, peeled and deveined
- 2 tablespoons olive oil
- 3 garlic cloves, minced
- 1-1/2 cups chopped fresh tomatoes
- 1 tablespoon minced chives
- 1 tablespoon minced fresh flat-leaf parsley
- 1 tablespoon minced fresh tarragon *or* 1 teaspoon dried tarragon
- 1 teaspoon dried chervil
- 3/4 teaspoon salt
- 1/4 teaspoon pepper
- 2 tablespoons butter, cubed

In a large nonstick skillet coated with cooking spray, cook shrimp in oil for 2 minutes. Add garlic; cook 1 minute longer.

Stir in the tomatoes and seasonings. Cook 3-5 minutes longer or until shrimp turn pink. Stir in butter until melted. **yield: 4 servings.**

oregano chicken

Taste of Home Test Kitchen

It's so easy to prepare this poultry mainstay created by our home economists. The handful of basic seasonings makes these chicken breasts a real treat. For faster cleanup, line your baking pan with foil.

- 2 bone-in chicken breast halves (10 ounces *each*)
- 3/4 teaspoon crushed garlic
- 3/4 teaspoon lemon-pepper seasoning
- 1/2 teaspoon dried oregano
- 1 tablespoon olive oil

Rub chicken with garlic; sprinkle with lemon-pepper and oregano. In a large skillet over medium heat, brown chicken, skin side down, in oil for 5 minutes.

Transfer to a shallow baking pan. Bake, uncovered, at 400° for 30-35 minutes or until a meat thermometer reads 170°. **yield: 2 servings.**

sausage rice casserole

sausage rice casserole

Eleanor Deaver • Fresno, California
The key to this bakes' distinctive flavor is using Italian sausage.
The balance of ingredients lends old-fashioned taste to this
just-right-for-two dish.

1/2	pound bulk Italian sausage
1/4	cup chopped onion
1/4	cup chopped sweet red pepper
1/2	cup uncooked instant rice
1/4	teaspoon dried basil
1	can (10-3/4 ounces) condensed tomato soup, undiluted
1/4	cup water
1/4	cup plus 2 tablespoons shredded part-skim mozzarella cheese, *divided*

In a small skillet, cook the sausage, onion and red pepper over medium heat until sausage is no longer pink; drain. Remove from the heat. Stir in the rice, basil, soup, water and 1/4 cup mozzarella cheese.

Transfer mixture to an ungreased 3-cup baking dish. Cover and bake at 350° for 25-30 minutes or until rice is tender. Uncover; sprinkle with remaining mozzarella cheese. Bake 5 minutes longer or until the cheese is melted. **yield: 2 servings.**

turkey leg pot roast

Rick and Vegas Pearson • Cadillac, Michigan
Well-seasoned turkey legs and tender veggies make this meal ideal for a crisp fall day. Moist and satisfying, this recipe couldn't be more comforting!

3	medium potatoes, peeled and quartered
2	cups fresh baby carrots
2	celery ribs, cut into 2-1/2-inch pieces
1	medium onion, peeled and quartered
3	garlic cloves, peeled and quartered

1/2	cup chicken broth
3	turkey drumsticks (8 ounces *each*), skin removed
2	teaspoons seasoned salt
1	teaspoon dried thyme
1	teaspoon dried parsley flakes
1/4	teaspoon pepper

In a greased 5-qt. slow cooker, combine the first six ingredients. Place drumsticks over vegetables. Sprinkle with the seasoned salt, thyme, parsley and pepper. Cover; cook on low for 5 to 5-1/2 hours or until a meat thermometer reads 180°. **yield: 3 servings.**

glazed ham with sweet potatoes

Eloise Smith • Willowbrook, Illinois
I took a class on cooking for singles. This recipe is the perfect size, and I can reheat the second serving the next day.

2	tablespoons apricot jam
1	teaspoon Dijon mustard
1	boneless fully cooked ham steak (about 8 ounces)
1	can (15-3/4 ounces) sweet potatoes, drained
1	can (8-1/2 ounces) sliced peaches, drained
2	tablespoons maple syrup, *divided*

In a small microwave-safe bowl, combine apricot jam and Dijon mustard. Microwave, uncovered, on high for 15-30 seconds or until the jam is melted; stir until blended. Set aside.

Place ham steak in an ovenproof skillet. Arrange sweet potatoes and peaches around ham. Drizzle with 1 tablespoon syrup. Broil 3-4 in. from the heat for 5 minutes. Turn ham, peaches and potatoes. Brush ham with jam mixture; drizzle peaches and potatoes with remaining syrup. Broil 5 minutes longer or until heated through. **yield: 2 servings.**

glazed ham with sweet potatoes

indonesian pork

southwest corn bread bake

Duane and Christine Geyer • Coralville, Iowa
Warm up chilly nights with this tasty casserole. It's loaded with hearty beans and corn, then topped with a from-scratch corn bread. For a crowd, I double the ingredients and bake it in a 9-in. x 13-in. baking dish for a bit longer.

- 1 can (16 ounces) chili beans, undrained
- 1 can (8-3/4 ounces) whole kernel corn, drained
- 2 tablespoons chopped onion
- 1/2 teaspoon ground cumin
- 1/2 cup all-purpose flour
- 1/2 cup cornmeal
- 2 tablespoons sugar
- 1-1/4 teaspoons baking powder
- 1/4 teaspoon salt
- 1/2 cup plus 1 tablespoon milk
- 1-1/2 teaspoons canola oil

In a large bowl, combine the chili beans, corn, onion and cumin. Transfer to an 8-in. square baking dish coated with cooking spray.

In another bowl, combine the flour, cornmeal, sugar, baking powder and salt. Combine milk and oil; stir into the dry ingredients just until moistened.

Drop by tablespoons over chili mixture; carefully spread over the top. Bake, uncovered, at 350° for 20-25 minutes or until golden brown. **yield: 4 servings.**

indonesian pork

Jan Stenze • Littleton, Colorado
A zippy marinade coats these pork kabobs perfectly. The recipe came from my mom, and it's one of our favorites.

- 2 tablespoons reduced-sodium soy sauce
- 1 tablespoon water
- 1 tablespoon lemon juice
- 1/2 cup chopped onion
- 1/3 cup salted peanuts
- 2 teaspoons ground coriander
- 2 teaspoons brown sugar
- 1 garlic clove, minced
- 1/4 teaspoon crushed red pepper flakes
- 1/8 teaspoon pepper
- 2 tablespoons butter, melted
- 1/2 cup chicken broth
- 2 boneless pork loin chops (1 inch thick and 5 ounces *each*), cut into 1-inch cubes

In a blender, combine the first 10 ingredients; cover and process until blended. Transfer to a small saucepan; stir in butter and broth. Bring to a boil; remove from the heat. Cool.

Pour the marinade into a large resealable plastic bag; add pork. Seal bag and turn to coat; refrigerate for 6 hours or overnight.

Drain and discard the marinade. Thread the pork cubes onto four small metal or soaked wooden skewers. Grill, uncovered, over medium heat for 12-14 minutes, turning occasionally, or until juices run clear. **yield: 2 servings.**

southwest corn bread bake

orange pork chops

Erika Niehoff • Eveleth, Minnesota
These pork chops are so easy to prepare and have a nice not-too-sweet flavor. The original recipe came from my dad, so it's a family tradition.

- 4 boneless pork loin chops (3/4 inch thick and 5 ounces *each*)
- 1/4 teaspoon salt
- 1/8 teaspoon pepper
- 1 garlic clove, minced
- 1 can (6 ounces) frozen orange juice concentrate, thawed
- 1/2 cup reduced-sodium chicken broth
- 1-1/2 teaspoons Worcestershire sauce
- 2 cups cooked brown rice

Sprinkle both sides of pork chops with salt and pepper. In a nonstick skillet coated with cooking spray, cook chops for 3-4 minutes on each side or until browned.

Transfer the pork chops to an 8-in. square baking dish coated with cooking spray. In the same skillet, cook garlic for 1 minute. Stir in the orange juice concentrate, broth and Worcestershire sauce; bring to a boil. Remove from the heat.

Pour 1/4 cup sauce over pork. Bake, uncovered, at 350° for 20-25 minutes or until a meat thermometer reads 160°, basting twice with sauce.

Bring the remaining sauce to a boil. Reduce heat; simmer, uncovered, for 5 minutes or until sauce is reduced to 1/2 cup. Serve pork chops with sauce and rice. **yield: 4 servings.**

orange pork chops

african beef curry

african beef curry

Heather Ewald • Bothnell, Washington
This is a popular dish with my family and friends. It's from my Aunt Linda, who was a missionary in Nigeria for 45 years. The stew is served on a bed of rice and sprinkled with toppings. I put the bowls of toppings on my large turntable, and everyone can take whatever they want. In addition to the coconut, peanuts and raisins, you could also top the stew with chopped cucumbers, pineapple tidbits or mandarin orange slices.

- 1 pound beef stew meat, cut into 1/2-inch cubes
- 1 can (14-1/2 ounces) diced tomatoes, undrained
- 1 small onion, chopped
- 1 small sweet red pepper, chopped
- 1 small green pepper, chopped
- 1 to 2 tablespoons curry powder
- 1/2 teaspoon salt
- Hot cooked rice
- Raisins, chopped salted peanuts and flaked coconut, optional

In a large saucepan, combine first seven ingredients. Bring to a boil. Reduce heat; cover and simmer for 1-1/2 to 2 hours or until meat is tender.

Serve with rice. Garnish with raisins, peanuts and flaked coconut if desired. **yield: 4 servings.**

Karen Hall
South Hamilton,
Massachusetts
*I add chicken to a few
pantry staples and have a
wonderful warm entree in
minutes. Guests always
request the recipe, but my
"pasta-hating husband" just
ask for seconds!*

lemon chicken with pasta

1-1/2	**cups uncooked medium pasta shells**
1/4	**cup dry bread crumbs**
1	**teaspoon garlic powder**
1/2	**teaspoon salt**
1/2	**teaspoon pepper**
1	**pound boneless skinless chicken breasts, cubed**
6	**teaspoons canola oil, *divided***
1	**medium onion, chopped**
2	**tablespoons all-purpose flour**
1	**cup reduced-sodium chicken broth**
1/4	**cup lemon juice**
1/4	**cup shredded Parmesan cheese**

Cook pasta according to package directions. Meanwhile, in a large resealable plastic bag, combine the bread crumbs, garlic powder, salt and pepper. Add chicken, a few pieces at a time, and shake to coat.

In a large nonstick skillet coated with cooking spray, saute the chicken in 4 teaspoons oil until juices run clear. Remove and keep warm.

In the same skillet, cook onion in remaining oil over medium heat until tender. Sprinkle with flour; stir until blended. Gradually stir in the chicken broth and lemon juice. Bring to a boil; cook and stir for 2 minutes or until the suace is thickened.

Drain pasta; toss with lemon sauce. Serve with chicken; sprinkle with cheese. **yield: 4 servings.**

phyllo-wrapped halibut

Carrie Vazzano • Rolling Meadows, Illinois

I created this easy entree to convince my husband that seafood doesn't have to taste "fishy." He likes the flaky, phyllo wrapping as well as the bright green and red vegetables hidden inside of it.

4	cups fresh baby spinach
3/4	cup chopped sweet red pepper
3/4	teaspoon salt-free lemon-pepper seasoning, *divided*
1/2	teaspoon lemon juice
6	sheets phyllo dough (14 inches x 9 inches)
2	tablespoons reduced-fat butter, melted
2	halibut fillets (4 ounces *each*)
1/4	teaspoon salt
1/8	teaspoon pepper
1/4	cup shredded part-skim mozzarella cheese

In a large nonstick skillet lightly coated with cooking spray, saute spinach and red pepper until tender. Add 1/2 teaspoon lemon-pepper and lemon juice. Remove from the heat; cool.

Line a baking sheet with foil and coat the foil with cooking spray; set aside. Place one sheet of phyllo dough on a work surface; brush with butter. (Until ready to use, keep phyllo dough covered with plastic wrap and a damp towel to prevent it from drying out.) Layer remaining phyllo over first sheet, brushing each with butter. Cut stack in half widthwise.

Place a halibut fillet in the center of each square; sprinkle with salt and pepper. Top with cheese and spinach mixture. Fold sides and bottom edge over fillet

and roll up to enclose it; trim end of phyllo if necessary. Brush with remaining butter; sprinkle with remaining lemon-pepper.

Place fillets seam side down on prepared baking sheet. Bake at 375° for 20-25 minutes or until golden brown. **yield: 2 servings.**

Editor's Note: This recipe was tested with Land O'Lakes light stick butter.

turkey stir-fry

Mildred Sherrer • Fort Worth, Texas

Need a nourishing dinner in minutes? Toss together these seven ingredients for a colorful and delicious main dish the whole family will love. Frozen veggies make it extra quick, and a garnish of fresh cilantro adds extra flavor.

1	pound turkey breast tenderloins, cubed
1	tablespoon canola oil
1	package (16 ounces) frozen stir-fry vegetable blend
1	medium onion, cut into wedges
1/2	cup stir-fry sauce
1/3	cup shredded carrot

Hot cooked rice

In a large skillet or wok, stir-fry turkey breast tenderloins in oil for 3-4 minutes or until no longer pink. Remove with a slotted spoon.

Stir-fry the mixed vegetables, onion, stir-fry sauce and shredded carrot for 4-6 minutes or until vegetables are tender. Add the turkey; heat through. Serve turkey and vegetables with rice. **yield: 4 servings.**

pasta with sausage 'n' peppers

pasta with sausage 'n' peppers

Janice Mitchell • Aurora, Colorado
I found this recipe years ago in an old Italian cookbook and made a few changes to it. It's been a regular on our dinner table ever since.

4	ounces uncooked angel hair pasta
1/2	pound bulk Italian sausage
1/2	cup chopped onion
1/2	medium green pepper, coarsely chopped
1/2	medium sweet red pepper, coarsely chopped
1	small garlic clove, minced
1-1/2	teaspoons all-purpose flour
1/2	cup half-and-half cream
2	tablespoons minced fresh parsley
1/2	teaspoon dried marjoram
1/4	teaspoon salt
1/8	teaspoon pepper
1/4	cup shredded Parmesan cheese

Cook angel hair pasta according to package directions. Meanwhile, in a large skillet, cook sausage and onion over medium heat until meat is no longer pink; drain. Stir in the peppers; cook 4-6 minutes longer or until peppers are tender. Add garlic; cook for 1 minute.

Combine the flour and half-and-half cream until smooth. Gradually stir into skillet. Bring to a boil; cook and stir for 2 minutes or until thickened. Stir in the parsley, marjoram, salt and pepper.

Drain pasta. Top with sausage mixture; toss to coat. Sprinkle with Parmesan cheese. **yield: 2 servings.**

ham and spaetzle bake

Taste of Home Test Kitchen
Tired of the same old ham and scalloped potatoes? Try this yummy and comforting change of pace from our home economists. Creamy and cheesy, the hearty one-dish meal goes together in just a few minutes using convenient deli (or leftover) ham.

3/4	cup uncooked spaetzle
1/3	cup finely chopped onion
2	teaspoons butter
2	teaspoons all-purpose flour
1/2	cup 2% milk
3/4	cup fresh broccoli florets
1/3	cup shredded Gruyere cheese
1/3	cup cubed deli ham
1/2	teaspoon ground mustard
1/8	teaspoon pepper

Cook spaetzle according to package directions. Meanwhile, in a small saucepan, saute onion in butter until tender. Stir in flour; gradually add milk. Bring to a boil; cook and stir for 2 minutes or until thickened. Remove from the heat.

Drain spaetzle; stir the spaetzle, broccoli, cheese, ham, mustard and pepper into the white sauce. Transfer to a 3-cup baking dish coated with cooking spray.

Bake, uncovered, at 375° for 15-18 minutes or until bubbly. **yield: 2 servings.**

ham and spaetzle bake

cranberry pork tenderloin

Betty Helton • Melbourne, Florida

I rely on a can of cranberry sauce to create the sweet sauce for this tender pork entree. I add orange juice and ground cloves to the mixture to season it nicely as it simmers.

- 1 pork tenderloin (1 pound)
- 1 can (14 ounces) whole-berry cranberry sauce
- 1/2 cup orange juice
- 1/4 cup sugar
- 1 tablespoon brown sugar
- 1 teaspoon ground mustard
- 1/4 to 1/2 teaspoon ground cloves
- 2 tablespoons cornstarch
- 3 tablespoons cold water

Place the tenderloin in a 3-qt. slow cooker. In a small bowl, combine the cranberry sauce, orange juice, sugars, mustard and cloves; pour over pork. Cover and cook on low for 5-6 hours or until a meat thermometer reads 160°.

Remove pork and keep warm. In a small bowl, combine cornstarch and cold water until smooth; gradually stir into cranberry mixture. Cover and cook on high for 15 minutes longer or until thickened. Serve with pork. **yield: 4 servings.**

nutty salmon

cranberry pork tenderloin

nutty salmon

Vicki Ruiz • Twin Falls, Idaho

I've been making this super-fast microwave dish for several years. It couldn't be easier or more delicious, and I always get compliments…even from people who don't normally like fish! Any leftovers make great salmon patties the next day.

- 1/2 cup slivered almonds
- 1/4 cup butter, cubed
- 1/4 cup lemon juice
- 1/4 teaspoon salt
- 1/8 teaspoon pepper
- 1-1/2 pounds salmon fillets

Place the almonds in a small microwave-safe bowl; add butter if desired. Cover and microwave on high for 3-4 minutes or until almonds are browned, stirring twice. Add the lemon juice, salt and pepper.

Place the salmon fillets in an 8-in. square microwave-safe dish; top with the almond mixture. Cover dish and microwave on high for 5-7 minutes or until the fish flakes easily with a fork. Let the fish stand for 5 minutes before serving. **yield: 4 servings.**

Editor's Note: This recipe was tested in a 1,100-watt microwave.

swedish meatballs

Taste of Home Test Kitchen

Our home economists agree, nutmeg, allspice and cardamom lend to the traditional taste of these moist meatballs. The creamy sauce has a rich beef flavor with a touch of dill.

1/2	cup soft bread crumbs
1	medium onion, chopped
1	egg, lightly beaten
2	tablespoons heavy whipping cream
1/2	teaspoon salt
1/8	teaspoon ground nutmeg
1/8	teaspoon ground allspice
1/8	teaspoon ground cardamom
3/4	pound lean ground beef (90% lean)
1/2	pound ground pork

GRAVY:

2	tablespoons butter
2	tablespoons all-purpose flour
1	cup beef broth
1/2	cup heavy whipping cream
1/4	teaspoon dill weed
1/4	cup minced fresh parsley, optional

In a large bowl, combine the first eight ingredients. Crumble beef and pork over mixture and mix well. Shape into 1-1/2-in. meatballs. Place meatballs on a greased rack in a shallow baking pan. Bake at 400° for 11-12 minutes or until no longer pink; drain.

Meanwhile, in a large saucepan, melt butter. Stir in flour until smooth; gradually add broth. Bring to a boil; cook and stir for 1-2 minutes or until thickened. Stir in cream and dill; simmer for 1 minute. Place meatballs in a serving dish; pour gravy over top. Garnish with parsley if desired. **yield: 4 servings.**

swedish meatballs

apricot chicken pasta

apricot chicken pasta

Elaine Sweet • Dallas, Texas

To come up with this pasta dish, I combined two of my husband's favorite things—apricots and chicken. It's not only scrumptious but a snap to prepare, too.

1/4	cup dried apricots, cut into thin strips
4-1/2	teaspoons sherry *or* reduced-sodium chicken broth
1	cup uncooked bow tie pasta
1/4	cup chopped fresh mushrooms
1-1/2	teaspoons olive oil
2	garlic cloves, minced
1	cup shredded cooked chicken breast
1/2	cup heavy whipping cream
2-1/4	teaspoons reduced-sodium soy sauce
1/4	cup crumbled Gorgonzola cheese
1/4	cup slivered almonds, toasted
1	green onion, chopped
1/4	teaspoon salt
1/4	teaspoon pepper

In a small saucepan, bring apricots and sherry to a boil. Reduce heat; simmer, uncovered, for 3 minutes or until apricots are tender. Cool.

Cook the bow tie pasta according to package directions. Meanwhile, in a large skillet, saute mushrooms in oil until tender. Add garlic; saute 1 minute longer. Reduce heat to medium. Add the chicken, whipping cream and soy sauce; cook and stir for 5 minutes.

Remove from the heat. Stir in the cheese, almonds, onion, salt, pepper and apricots. Drain pasta; toss with chicken mixture. **yield: 2 servings.**

salisbury steak with portobello sauce

*Taste of Home
Test Kitchen*

*Looking for an easy way to
turn Salisbury steak into
something extra special?
Dress up lean ground beef
patties with this flavorful
sauce from our home
economists made with wine,
shallots and mushrooms.*

salisbury steak with portobello sauce

3/4 **pound lean ground beef
(90% lean)**
1/4 **teaspoon salt**
1/8 **teaspoon pepper**
3 **tablespoons port wine *or* beef
broth**
2 **tablespoons chopped shallots**
1-1/2 **teaspoons balsamic vinegar**
1/2 **cup sliced baby portobello
mushrooms**
1-1/2 **teaspoons all-purpose flour**
1/2 **cup beef broth**
1 **teaspoon Worcestershire sauce**
1 **teaspoon ketchup**
1/8 **teaspoon dried rosemary, crushed**

In a large bowl, combine the beef, salt and pepper; shape into two oval patties. In a large skillet, cook patties over medium heat until no longer pink.

Meanwhile, in a small saucepan, combine the wine, shallots and vinegar. Bring to a boil; cook for 5 minutes or until thickened.

Toss the mushrooms with flour; add to saucepan. Stir in the broth, Worcestershire sauce, ketchup and rosemary. Bring to a boil; cook and stir for 3-5 minutes or until mushrooms are tender. Drain patties; serve with sauce. **yield: 2 servings.**

hearty chicken-filled potato

Janet Dingler • Cedartown, Georgia
Try one of these colorful, over-stuffed spuds with all the fixings and Southwest flavor of fajitas. All that's missing are the tortillas and the messy eating!

- 1 large baking potato
- 1/4 teaspoon ground cumin
- 1/8 teaspoon dried oregano
- 1/4 teaspoon salt, *divided*

Dash cayenne pepper

- 1 boneless skinless chicken breast half (4 ounces)
- 1 teaspoon butter, softened
- 1/4 cup shredded Mexican cheese blend *or* cheddar cheese
- 2 tablespoons sour cream
- 1-1/2 teaspoons milk

Dash pepper

Salsa, minced fresh cilantro, minced chives and additional sour cream, optional

Scrub and pierce potato. Bake at 375° for 1 hour or until tender. Meanwhile, combine the cumin, oregano, 1/8 teaspoon salt and cayenne; rub over chicken. Place chicken in a small baking dish coated with cooking spray. Bake, uncovered, at 375° for 20-25 minutes or until the juices run clear.

Cut chicken into small cubes; set aside. When cool enough to handle, cut a thin slice off the top of potato and discard. Scoop out pulp, leaving a thin shell. In a

hearty chicken-filled potato

crispy cod with veggies

small bowl, mash the pulp with butter. Stir in cheese, sour cream, milk, pepper, remaining salt and chicken.

Spoon into potato shell. Place on an ungreased baking sheet. Bake at 375° for 10-15 minutes or until heated through. Garnish with salsa, cilantro, chives and additional sour cream if desired. **yield: 1 serving.**

crispy cod with veggies

Taste of Home Test Kitchen
Take the chill off brisk evenings and warm the body and soul with this light but nourishing entree from our home economists. Round out the meal with a loaf of crusty bread.

- 2 cups broccoli coleslaw mix
- 1/2 cup chopped fresh tomato
- 4 teaspoons chopped green onion
- 2 garlic cloves, minced
- 2 cod fillets (6 ounces *each*)

Pepper to taste

- 1/4 cup crushed potato sticks
- 3 tablespoons seasoned bread crumbs
- 2 tablespoons grated Parmesan cheese
- 4 teaspoons butter, melted

In a large bowl, combine the coleslaw mix, tomato, onion and garlic; spread into an 11-in. x 7-in. baking pan coated with cooking spray. Top with cod fillets; sprinkle with pepper.

Combine the potato sticks, bread crumbs, cheese and butter; sprinkle over fillets. Bake, uncovered, at 450° for 25-30 minutes or until fish flakes easily with a fork. **yield: 2 servings.**

desserts

There's always room for dessert—especially when it's made for a pair. Satisfy your sweet tooth with this scrumptious selection of pies, cakes and other indulgences fit for two.

turtle cheesecake, page 105

Raymonde Bourgeois
Swastika, Ontario

Meringues can be challenging to some home bakers. If you're really craving this dessert, you can purchase them at your favorite bakery. Add this sweet sauce, and you're all set!

cocoa meringues with berries

1	**egg white**
1/8	**teaspoon cream of tartar**
Dash salt	
3	**tablespoons sugar,** *divided*
1	**tablespoon baking cocoa**
1/4	**teaspoon vanilla extract**
2	**tablespoons finely chopped bittersweet chocolate**

BERRY SAUCE:

2	**tablespoons sugar**
1	**teaspoon cornstarch**
2	**tablespoons orange juice**
1	**tablespoon water**
1/2	**cup fresh** *or* **frozen blueberries, thawed**
1/2	**cup fresh** *or* **frozen raspberries, thawed**

Place egg white in a small bowl; let stand at room temperature for 30 minutes. Add cream of tartar and salt; beat on medium speed until soft peaks form. Gradually beat in 2 tablespoons sugar.

Combine cocoa and remaining sugar; add to meringue with vanilla. Beat on high until stiff glossy peaks form and sugar is dissolved. Fold in chopped chocolate.

Drop two mounds onto a parchment paper-lined baking sheet. Shape into 3-in. cups with the back of a spoon. Bake at 275° for 50-60 minutes or until set and dry. Turn oven off; leave the meringues in the oven for 1 hour.

In a small saucepan, combine the sugar, cornstarch, orange juice and water. Bring to a boil; cook and stir for 1 minute or until thickened. Remove from the heat; stir in berries. Cool to room temperature. Spoon into meringues. **yield: 2 servings.**

maple pumpkin pie

Vivian Colwell • Goshen, Ohio

Here's a 5-inch pie that's as cute as it is delectable. You'll enjoy the seasonal pumpkin-maple filling and golden, melt-in-your-mouth crust. It's especially good with whipped cream.

- 1/2   cup all-purpose flour
- 1/8   teaspoon salt
- 2   tablespoons shortening
- 2   tablespoons cold water

FILLING:

- 1/2   cup canned pumpkin
- 1/3   cup evaporated milk
- 1/4   cup packed brown sugar
- 1   egg
- 2   teaspoons sugar
- 1/2   teaspoon pumpkin pie spice
- 1/2   teaspoon maple flavoring

Dash salt

In a small bowl, combine flour and salt; cut in shortening until crumbly. Gradually add water, tossing with a fork until dough forms a ball. Cover and refrigerate for 15 minutes or until easy to handle. Meanwhile, in a small bowl, combine the filling ingredients.

On a lightly floured surface, roll out dough to fit a 5-in. pie plate. Transfer the pastry to pie plate. Trim to 1/2 in. beyond edge of plate; flute edges. Pour the filling into crust.

Bake at 375° for 40-45 minutes or until a knife inserted near the center comes out clean. Cool on a wire rack. Store in the refrigerator. **yield: 2 servings.**

tiramisu for two

tiramisu for two

Barbara Lopshire • Holland, Michigan

This mouthwatering confection for two is a combination of four or five different recipes. Sometimes, I make it in a loaf pan instead of individual dishes and use Kahlua or Godiva liqueur in place of the chocolate syrup.

- 6   ladyfingers, split
- 2   tablespoons brewed coffee, *divided*
- 1/2   cup (4 ounces) Mascarpone cheese
- 1/4   cup confectioners' sugar
- 1   tablespoon chocolate syrup
- 1/2   cup heavy whipping cream
- 1   tablespoon baking cocoa

Line the bottoms and sides of two 8-oz. ramekins or custard cups with ladyfingers, arranging them to resemble a spoke pattern. Brush with 1 tablespoon coffee; set aside.

In a small bowl, beat Mascarpone cheese and confectioners' sugar until smooth; beat in chocolate syrup on low speed.

In another small bowl, beat cream until stiff peaks form; fold into cheese mixture. Spoon into ramekins; drizzle with remaining coffee. Dust with cocoa. Refrigerate until serving. **yield: 2 servings.**

maple pumpkin pie

roasted pears in pecan sauce

Darlene King • Estevan, Saskatchewan
Whenever I bring home pears from the store, my family begs me to make this after-dinner treat. They absolutely love the tender autumn fruit smothered in a sweet and creamy pecan sauce. We find it's simply luscious over ice cream and cake.

- 4   medium pears, peeled and cut into wedges
- 3   tablespoons brown sugar
- 3   tablespoons unsweetened apple juice
- 3   tablespoons butter, melted
- 1/4 cup chopped pecans
- 3   tablespoons heavy whipping cream

Vanilla ice cream, optional

Place pears in an ungreased 13-in. x 9-in. baking dish. In a small bowl, combine the brown sugar, apple juice and butter; pour over pears. Bake, uncovered, at 400° for 20 minutes, basting occasionally.

Sprinkle with pecans. Bake 10-15 minutes longer or until pears are tender. Transfer pears to serving dishes.

Pour cooking juices into a small bowl; whisk in cream until blended. Drizzle over pears. Serve with ice cream if desired. **yield: 4 servings.**

minty baked alaska

Brenda Mast • Clearwater, Florida
I've made this dessert on a few special occasions for my husband and me. He just loves it. It's so simple, but it looks and tastes like you spent all day in the kitchen. Crushed peppermint candy adds a unique taste and decorative touch to this finale that never fails to impress.

- 2   egg whites
- 1/4 cup sugar
- 1/4 teaspoon cream of tartar
- 1/4 teaspoon vanilla extract

Dash salt

- 1   tablespoon crushed peppermint candy
- 2   individual round sponge cakes
- 2/3 cup mint chocolate chip ice cream

In a small heavy saucepan, combine the egg whites, sugar and cream of tartar. With a hand mixer, beat on low speed for 1 minute. Continue beating over low heat until egg mixture reaches 160°, about 12 minutes.

minty baked alaska

Remove from the heat. Add vanilla and salt; beat until stiff glossy peaks form and sugar is dissolved. Fold in peppermint candy.

Place sponge cakes on an ungreased foil-lined baking sheet. Top each with 1/3 cup mint chocolate chip ice cream. Immediately spread meringue over ice cream and cake, sealing it to foil on sheet. Broil 8 in. from heat for 3-5 minutes or until lightly browned. Serve immediately. **yield: 2 servings.**

grilled peach crisps for 2

Michelle Sandoval • Escalon, California
Most of the fat and sugar is eliminated from this grilled version of peach cobbler. It's a perfect finish to a summer barbecue.

- 1/2 teaspoon sugar
- 1/8 teaspoon ground cinnamon
- 1   medium peach, halved and pitted
- 1   cup reduced-fat vanilla ice cream
- 1/4 cup reduced-fat granola

In a small bowl, combine sugar and cinnamon; sprinkle over cut sides of peach. Let stand for 5 minutes.

Using long-handled tongs, moisten a paper towel with cooking oil and lightly coat the grill rack. Place peach cut side down on grill rack. Grill, covered, over medium heat for 8-10 minutes or until peach is tender and begins to caramelize. Place peach halves in dessert bowls. Serve with ice cream and granola. **yield: 2 servings.**

eggnog banana cream pies

eggnog banana
cream pies

Mary Ann Dell • *Phoenixville, Pennsylvania*
This pie is a delicious dessert on any occasion and one of our family's favorites. It is one of my mother's recipes, who was a fabulous baker and cook.

- 21 reduced-fat vanilla wafers
- 1 small banana, sliced
- 1/4 teaspoon ground nutmeg
- 1 cup fat-free milk
- 2 tablespoons plus 1 teaspoon sugar-free instant vanilla pudding mix
- 4 ounces fat-free cream cheese
- 1/4 teaspoon rum extract
- 1/2 cup fat-free whipped topping

GARNISH:
- 1 small banana, sliced
- 1/8 teaspoon ground nutmeg

Line three ungreased 5-in. pie plates with vanilla wafers. Arrange banana slices over bottom of crusts; sprinkle with nutmeg. Set aside.

In a small bowl, whisk milk and pudding mix for 2 minutes. In another bowl, beat cream cheese until smooth. Add pudding and rum extract; beat on low speed until blended. Fold in whipped topping. Spoon over banana.

Cover; refrigerate pies for 1 hour before serving. Just before serving, garnish pies with banana and nutmeg. **yield: 3 servings.**

chocolate malted
bread pudding

Roxanne Chan • *Albany, California*
Some leftover bread, an open can of chocolate syrup and a package of malted milk balls inspired this yummy recipe. Adding almonds gives the pudding a pleasing crunch.

- 1 cup cubed day-old bread
- 1/4 cup coarsely chopped malted milk balls
- 3 tablespoons semisweet chocolate chips
- 2 tablespoons sliced almonds, toasted
- 1 tablespoon chocolate syrup
- 1/2 cup 2% milk
- 2 tablespoons cream cheese, softened
- 1 egg
- 2 tablespoons malted milk powder

Whipped cream, optional

Place the bread cubes in two 8-oz. ramekins coated with cooking spray; sprinkle with malted milk balls, semisweet chocolate chips and sliced almonds. Drizzle with chocolate syrup.

In a blender, combine the milk, cream cheese, egg and malted milk powder; cover and process until smooth. Pour over bread cube mixture. Let stand for 15 minutes.

Bake at 325° for 25-30 minutes or until mixture reaches 160°. Cool for 10 minutes before serving. Dollop with whipped cream if desired. **yield: 2 servings.**

chocolate malted bread pudding

cranberry cheesecake tartlets

cranberry cheesecake tartlets

Taste of Home Test Kitchen

Ordinary cranberry sauce becomes extraordinary when spooned on top of a cheesecake filling inside a nutty crust. Individual servings make this treat very distinctive.

- 1 cup slivered almonds, toasted
- 1/4 cup all-purpose flour
- 3 tablespoons sugar
- 1/4 cup cold butter, cubed
- 2 packages (3 ounces *each*) cream cheese, softened
- 1/4 cup confectioners' sugar
- 2 tablespoons lemon juice
- 1 cup whipped topping
- 1 cup whole-berry cranberry sauce

In a food processor, combine the almonds, flour and sugar; cover and process until blended. Add butter; cover and process until mixture forms coarse crumbs.

Press onto the bottom and up the sides of four greased 4-in. tart pans with removable bottoms. Bake at 350° for 13-15 minutes or until golden brown. Let crusts cool completely on a wire rack.

In a small bowl, beat cream cheese until smooth. Add confectioners' sugar and lemon juice until and mix well. Fold in whipped topping.

Spoon into crusts. Cover and refrigerate for 4 hours or until set. Just before serving, top with cranberry sauce. **yield: 4 servings.**

chocolate eclair graham dessert

Patricia Pruett • Pueblo West, Colorado

Here's a smaller and easier version of a sweet classic. The vanilla filling sets beautifully, complementing the graham cracker crust and luscious chocolate coating.

- 9 graham cracker squares
- 1/2 cup cold 2% milk
- 1/3 cup instant vanilla pudding mix
- 1/2 cup whipped topping

TOPPING:
- 1/2 ounce semisweet chocolate
- 1-1/2 teaspoons butter
- 2-1/4 teaspoons 2% milk
- 1-1/2 teaspoons light corn syrup
- 1/2 teaspoon vanilla extract
- 1/3 cup confectioners' sugar

Cut graham crackers in half, making 18 rectangles. Place nine rectangles in an ungreased 8-in. x 4-in. loaf pan; set aside.

In a small bowl, whisk milk and vanilla pudding mix for 2 minutes. Let stand for 2 minutes or until soft-set. Fold in whipped topping. Spread over graham crackers; top with remaining graham crackers.

For topping, microwave-safe bowl, melt chocolate and butter. Stir in the milk, corn syrup, vanilla and confectioners' sugar. Spread over graham crackers. Cover and refrigerate overnight. **yield: 4 servings.**

Editor's Note: We do not recommend substituting sugar-free pudding mix in this recipe.

chocolate eclair graham dessert

Theresa Sabbagh
Winston-Salem,
North Carolina
I love this recipe because
it's a tasty twist on my
all-time favorite
dessert…homemade
apple pie.

apple cream cheese tart

3	tablespoons butter, softened
3	tablespoons sugar
1/4	teaspoon vanilla extract
6	tablespoons all-purpose flour

FILLING:

1	package (3 ounces) cream cheese, softened
2	tablespoons beaten egg
1/4	teaspoon vanilla extract
2/3	cup thinly sliced peeled tart apple (1/8-inch slices)
2	teaspoons sugar
1/4	teaspoon ground cinnamon
2	tablespoons slivered almonds

Whipped cream and ground nutmeg, optional

In a small bowl, cream butter and sugar; beat in vanilla. Stir in flour. Press onto the bottom and 1 in. up the sides of a 6-in. springform pan coated with cooking spray; set aside.

For filling, in a small bowl, beat the cream cheese, egg and vanilla. Pour over crust. In a bowl, combine the apple, sugar and cinnamon; arrange over filling. Sprinkle with almonds.

Place pan on a baking sheet. Bake at 350° for 30-35 minutes or until apple slices are tender. Cool on a wire rack. Remove sides of pan. Garnish with whipped cream and nutmeg if desired. Refrigerate leftovers. **yield: 4 servings.**

chocolate malt cheesecake

Anna Ginsberg • Austin, Texas
With quite an impressive presentation and that classic malt flavor, this downsized sensation will make dinner extra special for any twosome.

- 4 portions refrigerated ready-to-bake sugar cookie dough
- 4 ounces cream cheese, softened
- 1/2 cup dark chocolate chips, melted
- 2 tablespoons sugar
- 1 egg white
- 1/2 teaspoon vanilla extract

TOPPING:
- 4-1/2 teaspoons cream cheese, softened
- 2 teaspoons sugar
- 1 teaspoon malted milk powder
- 1 teaspoon baking cocoa
- 2/3 cup whipped topping
- 1 tablespoon chocolate syrup

Line a 5-3/4-in. x 3-in. x 2-in. loaf pan with foil. Press cookie dough onto bottom of pan. Bake at 325° for 15-20 minutes or until golden brown. Cool on a wire rack.

In a small bowl, beat cream cheese, melted chocolate and sugar until smooth. Add egg white; beat on low speed just until combined. Stir in vanilla. Pour over the baked crust.

chocolate malt cheesecake

Place loaf pan in a baking pan; add 1 in. of hot water to larger pan. Bake at 325° for 40-45 minutes or until center is just set and top appears dull.

Remove loaf pan from water bath. Cool on a wire rack for 10 minutes. Carefully run a knife around edge of pan to loosen; cool 1 hour longer.

Refrigerate overnight. For topping, in a small bowl, beat the cream cheese, sugar, milk powder and baking cocoa until smooth. Fold in whipped topping. Spread over cheesecake. Cover and refrigerate for 1 hour.

Using foil, lift cheesecake out of pan. Cut in half. Drizzle chocolate syrup over each piece. Refrigerate leftovers. **yield: 2 servings.**

creamy flan

Amanda Pettit • Logan, Ohio
Flan, a traditional Southwestern confection, has always been a hit with my family and friends. For when I'm not feeding a crowd, I made it to be just enough for two. This scaled-back version is just as creamy and delicious as the original.

- 5 tablespoons sugar, *divided*
- 1 cup milk
- 1/3 cup egg substitute
- 1-1/2 teaspoons vanilla extract

In a small skillet over medium-low heat, cook 3 tablespoons sugar until melted, about 5 minutes. Do not stir. Reduce heat to low; cook for 5 minutes or until syrup is golden brown, stirring occasionally.

Quickly pour syrup into two ungreased 6-ounce custard cups or ramekins, tilting to coat bottom of dish. Let stand for 10 minutes.

In a small saucepan, heat milk until bubbles form around sides of saucepan. Remove from the heat.

In a small bowl, whisk egg substitute and remaining sugar. Stir half of the warm milk into egg mixture; return all to pan and mix well. Add vanilla. Slowly pour into prepared dishes.

Place dishes in a baking pan. Fill pan with boiling water to a depth of 3/4 in. Bake at 325° for 25-30 minutes or until center is just set (mixture will jiggle). Remove to a wire rack; cool for 1 hour. Refrigerate for at least 1 hour.

Run a knife around edge and invert each dish onto a small rimmed serving dish. Refrigerate any leftovers. **yield: 2 servings.**

rhubarb crisp

rhubarb crisp

Rosie Spieth • Albion, Indiana
Rhubarb and layers of spiced crumb topping make this delight perfect for spring. It's such a comforting ending to a meal.

  2 **cups diced fresh *or* frozen rhubarb**
1/3 **cup sugar**
1/3 **cup packed brown sugar**
1/4 **cup all-purpose flour**
1/4 **cup old-fashioned oats**
1/2 **teaspoon ground cinnamon**
1/4 **teaspoon ground nutmeg**
  2 **tablespoons cold butter**

In a small bowl, combine the rhubarb and sugar. In another bowl, combine the brown sugar, flour, oats, cinnamon and nutmeg; cut in butter until crumbly.

In two 10-oz. baking dishes or ramekins coated with cooking spray, layer half of the rhubarb mixture and half of the crumb mixture. Repeat layers. Bake, uncovered, at 375° for 20-25 minutes or until rhubarb is tender. **yield: 2 servings.**

Editor's Note: If using frozen rhubarb, measure rhubarb while still frozen, then thaw completely. Drain in a colander, but do not press liquid out.

chocolate mint souffles

Ruth Lee • Troy, Ontario
These delectable little desserts are fancy and utterly foolproof. It's the best way to showcase the mint and chocolate combo.

  2 **eggs**
  1 **teaspoon plus 4 tablespoons sugar, *divided***
  2 **tablespoons baking cocoa**
  1 **teaspoon cornstarch**
Dash salt
1/3 **cup fat-free milk**
  2 **tablespoons semisweet chocolate chips**
1/8 **teaspoon mint extract**
Confectioners' sugar

Separate eggs. Place whites in a small bowl; let stand at room temperature for 30 minutes. Place yolks in another bowl; set aside.

Coat two 10-oz. ramekins or custard cups with cooking spray and lightly sprinkle with 1 teaspoon sugar; place on a baking sheet and set aside.

In a saucepan over medium heat, combine 2 tablespoons sugar, cocoa, cornstarch and salt. Gradually stir in milk. Bring to a boil, stirring constantly. Cook and stir for 1-2 minutes or until thickened.

Remove from the heat; stir in chocolate chips and extract until chips are melted. Transfer to a small bowl. Stir a small amount of hot mixture into egg yolks; return all to the bowl, stirring constantly. Cool slightly.

Beat egg whites on medium speed until soft peaks form. Gradually beat in remaining sugar, 1 tablespoon at a time, on high until stiff peaks form. With a spatula, fold a fourth of the egg whites into chocolate mixture until no white streaks remain. Fold in remaining egg whites until combined.

Transfer to prepared ramekins. Bake at 375° for 18-22 minutes or until tops are puffed and centers are almost set. Sprinkle with confectioners' sugar. Serve immediately. **yield: 2 servings.**

chocolate mint souffles

white chocolate creme brulee

white chocolate creme brulee

Carole Resnick • Cleveland, Ohio
If you like creme brulee, you have to try this version. Dressed up with white chocolate, it's a special romantic treat.

- 3 egg yolks
- 6 tablespoons sugar, *divided*
- 1 cup heavy whipping cream
- 2 ounces white baking chocolate, finely chopped
- 1/4 teaspoon vanilla extract

In a small bowl, whisk egg yolks and 2 tablespoons sugar; set aside. In a small saucepan, combine the cream, chocolate and 2 tablespoons sugar. Heat over medium-low heat until chocolate is melted and mixture is smooth, stirring constantly.

Remove from the heat. Stir in vanilla. Stir a small amount of hot filling into egg yolk mixture; return all to the pan, stirring constantly.

Pour into two 10-oz. ramekins. Place in a baking pan. Add 1 in. of boiling water to pan. Bake, uncovered, at 325° for 50-55 minutes or until center is set. Remove from water bath. Cool for 10 minutes. Refrigerate for at least 4 hours.

If using a creme brulee torch, sprinkle with remaining sugar. Heat sugar with the torch until caramelized. Serve immediately.

If broiling the custards, place ramekins on a baking sheet; let stand at room temperature for 15 minutes. Sprinkle with remaining sugar. Broil 8 in. from the heat for 4-7 minutes or until sugar is caramelized. Refrigerate for 1-2 hours or until firm. **yield: 2 servings.**

fudgy peanut butter cake

Bonnie Evans • Norcross, Georgia
I clipped this recipe from a newspaper years ago. The house smells great while it's cooking. My husband and son enjoy this warm cake with vanilla ice cream and nuts on top.

- 1/3 cup milk
- 1/4 cup peanut butter
- 1 tablespoon canola oil
- 1/2 teaspoon vanilla extract
- 3/4 cup sugar, *divided*
- 1/2 cup all-purpose flour
- 3/4 teaspoon baking powder
- 2 tablespoons baking cocoa
- 1 cup boiling water

Vanilla ice cream

In a large bowl, combine the milk, peanut butter, oil and vanilla, beat until well blended. In a small bowl, combine 1/4 cup sugar, flour and baking powder; gradually beat into peanut butter mixture until blended. Spread evenly into a 1-1/2-qt. slow cooker coated with cooking spray.

In a small bowl, combine the baking cocoa and remaining sugar; stir in boiling water. Pour into the slow cooker (do not stir).

Cover and cook on high for 1-1/2 to 2 hours or until a toothpick inserted near the center of comes out clean. Serve warm with ice cream. **yield: 4 servings.**

Editor's Note: Reduced-fat or generic brands of peanut butter are not recommended for this recipe.

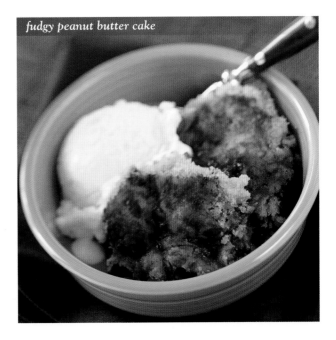
fudgy peanut butter cake

miniature spiced chocolate cakes

Taste of Home Test Kitchen

Our home economists created these individual chocolate delights that feature rich, tender cake and a smooth, velvety chocolate sauce. One bite is pure heaven. Set out two forks and share this dessert with the one you love!

- 2/3 **cup butter**
- 7 **ounces German sweet chocolate**
- 1/2 **teaspoon ground cardamom**
- 1/2 **teaspoon ground cinnamon**
- 1/8 **teaspoon white pepper**
- 1/8 **teaspoon ground cloves**
- 3 **eggs**
- 3 **egg yolks**
- 1/2 **teaspoon rum extract**
- 1/2 **teaspoon vanilla extract**
- 1-1/2 **cups confectioners' sugar**
- 1/2 **cup all-purpose flour**
- **Additional confectioners' sugar**
- **Hot fudge ice cream topping, warmed**

In a heavy saucepan over low heat, melt the butter, chocolate, cardamom, cinnamon, pepper and cloves; stir until smooth. Remove from the heat; cool for 5 minutes. In a large bowl, whisk the eggs, yolks and extracts. Whisk in chocolate mixture. Add confectioners' sugar and flour; whisk until blended.

Pour into four generously greased 6-oz. souffle dishes or custard cups to within 1/4 in. of the top. Place on a

sugar cookie tarts

baking sheet. Bake at 425° for 15-17 minutes or until a thermometer inserted near the center reads 160°.

Cool on a wire rack for 5 minutes. Remove cakes from dishes to dessert plates. Dust with confectioners' sugar and drizzle with fudge topping. Serve immediately. **yield: 4 servings.**

sugar cookie tarts

Barb White • Ligonier, Pennsylvania

Purchased sugar cookies serve as the speedy "crust" for these tasty tarts topped with cream cheese and fresh fruit.

- 5 **tablespoons sugar,** *divided*
- 1 **teaspoon cornstarch**
- **Dash salt**
- 3 **tablespoons water**
- 2 **tablespoons orange juice**
- 1 **tablespoon lemon juice**
- 1 **package (3 ounces) cream cheese, softened**
- 4 **large sugar cookies (3 inches)**
- 1 **cup sliced assorted fresh fruit (strawberries, kiwifruit** *and/or* **bananas)**

For glaze, in a small saucepan, combine 3 tablespoons sugar, cornstarch and salt. Gradually stir in the water, orange juice and lemon juice. Bring to a boil over medium heat; cook and stir for 2 minutes or until thickened. Remove from the heat; cool.

In a small bowl, beat cream cheese and remaining sugar until smooth. Spread over each cookie; arrange fruit on top. Drizzle with glaze. Refrigerate until chilled. **yield: 4 servings.**

miniature spiced chocolate cakes

Taste of Home Test Kitchen

This elegant after-dinner sensation, created by our home economists, lives up to its name. With pretty strawberries, a creamy filling and flaked coconut topping, it takes a little extra care to put together, but the results are well worth it.

spectacular strawberry dessert

1/4 cup butter, softened
2 tablespoons confectioners' sugar
1/4 teaspoon vanilla extract
1/2 cup all-purpose flour
Dash salt
FILLING:
1/4 cup sugar
2 teaspoons cornstarch
2 teaspoons all-purpose flour
Dash salt
3/4 cup 2% milk
1 egg yolk, lightly beaten
1 tablespoon butter
1/2 teaspoon vanilla extract
1-1/2 cups sliced fresh strawberries
TOPPING:
4 ounces cream cheese, softened
1/4 cup confectioners' sugar
4 tablespoons flaked coconut, divided
1/2 cup heavy whipping cream
Fresh mint and additional sliced strawberries, optional

In a small bowl, cream butter and confectioners' sugar until light and fluffy. Beat in vanilla. Combine flour and salt. Gradually add to creamed mixture and mix well. With lightly floured hands, press onto a 7-1/2-in. pizza pan; build up edges slightly. Bake at 350° for 12-15 minutes or until edges and bottom are lightly browned. Cool on a wire rack for 15 minutes.

In a small saucepan, combine the sugar, cornstarch, flour and salt. Gradually stir in milk until smooth. Cook and stir over medium heat until thickened and bubbly. Reduce heat; cook and stir 2 minutes longer. Remove from the heat. Gradually stir 2 tablespoons of hot filling into egg yolk; return all to the pan, stirring constantly. Bring to a gentle boil; cook and stir 2 minutes longer.

Remove from the heat. Gently stir in butter and vanilla. Cool for 30 minutes without stirring. Pour over crust. Top with strawberries.

In a small bowl, beat the cream cheese, confectioners' sugar and 2 tablespoons coconut until smooth. In another bowl, beat cream on medium speed until soft peaks form; fold into cream cheese mixture. Carefully spread over strawberries. Toast remaining coconut; sprinkle over topping. Garnish with mint and berries if desired. Chill for at least 4 hours. **yield: 4 servings.**

mini apple pie

mini apple pie

Edna Hoffman • *Hebron, Indiana*

I like to try new recipes when apples are in season. When I created this one, it was named a keeper. Golden Delicious apples are our favorites, so I bake up this little dessert regularly during the early fall.

1/4   **cup golden raisins**
1/3   **cup apple juice**
2   **large Golden Delicious apples (about 1 pound), peeled and sliced**
2   **tablespoons sugar**
2   **tablespoons brown sugar**
1   **tablespoon all-purpose flour**
1/4   **teaspoon ground cinnamon**
Pastry for single-crust pie (9 inches)

In a large saucepan over medium heat, cook raisins in apple juice for 5 minutes. Add apples; cook, uncovered, for 8-10 minutes or until tender. Remove apple mixture from the heat; let cool.

Combine the sugars, flour and cinnamon; add to apple mixture. On a floured surface, roll out half of the pastry to fit a 20-oz. baking dish. Place pastry in dish; trim to edge of dish. Add filling.

Roll out the remaining pastry to fit top of pie; place over filling. Trim, seal and flute edges. Cut slits in the top of the pastry.

Bake at 400° for 35-40 minutes or until golden brown and bubbly. Cool on a wire rack. **yield: 2 servings.**

blueberry crumble

Beth Tomlinson • *Streetsboro, Ohio*

This super-easy dessert features sweet blueberries with a crumbly topping that only gets better when topped with vanilla ice cream. Because it cooks in the microwave, it's ready to enjoy in minutes.

3   **cups fresh *or* frozen blueberries**
3   **tablespoons sugar**
1   **tablespoon cornstarch**
1/3   **cup old-fashioned oats**
1/3   **cup packed brown sugar**
3   **tablespoons all-purpose flour**
2   **tablespoons chopped almonds**
1/8   **teaspoon ground cinnamon**
3   **tablespoons cold butter**
Vanilla ice cream

In a greased 9-in. microwave-safe pie plate, combine the blueberries, sugar and cornstarch. Cover and microwave on high for 7-8 minutes or until thickened, stirring twice.

Meanwhile, in a small bowl, combine the oats, brown sugar, flour, almonds and cinnamon. Cut in butter until mixture resembles coarse crumbs. Sprinkle over blueberry mixture.

Microwave, uncovered, on high for 2-3 minutes or until the butter is melted. Serve crumble with vanilla ice cream. **yield: 4 servings.**

Editor's Note: This recipe was tested in a 1,100-watt microwave.

blueberry crumble

s'more ice cream pie

s'more ice cream pie

Taste of Home Test Kitchen

The next best thing to that classic campfire treat? Try this easy but elegant-looking freezer pie from our home economists. It melts in your mouth!

2/3 cup graham cracker crumbs
  2 tablespoons sugar
  3 tablespoons butter, melted
2-1/2 cups rocky road ice cream, softened
2/3 cup marshmallow creme
3/4 cup miniature marshmallows

In a small bowl, combine graham cracker crumbs and sugar; stir in butter. Press onto the bottom and up the sides of a 7-in. pie plate coated with cooking spray. Bake at 325° for 7-9 minutes or until lightly browned. Let crust cool on a wire rack.

Carefully spread ice cream into crust; freeze until firm. Spread marshmallow creme over ice cream. Top with marshmallows; gently press into creme. Cover and freeze for 4 hours or overnight.

Just before serving, broil 6 in. from the heat for 1-2 minutes or until the marshmallows are golden brown. **yield: 4 servings.**

tiny texas sheet cakes

Hope Meece • Ambia, Indiana

These tiny sheet cakes boast a homemade chocolate flavor as big as Texas itself. They are moist, freeze well unfrosted and always bring compliments.

1/4 cup butter, cubed
1/4 cup water
  1 tablespoon baking cocoa
1/2 cup all-purpose flour
1/2 cup sugar
1/2 teaspoon baking powder
1/4 teaspoon ground cinnamon
Dash salt
  2 tablespoons beaten egg
  2 tablespoons 2% milk
FROSTING:
  2 tablespoons butter
4-1/2 teaspoons 2% milk
  1 tablespoon baking cocoa
3/4 cup confectioners' sugar
1/4 teaspoon vanilla extract
  2 tablespoons chopped pecans, toasted, optional

In a large saucepan, bring butter, water and cocoa just to a boil. Immediately remove from the heat. Combine the flour, sugar, baking powder, cinnamon and salt; stir dry ingredients into butter mixture. Add egg and milk; mix well.

Pour into two 5-3/4-in. x 3-in. x 2-in. loaf pans coated with cooking spray. Bake at 350° for 20-25 minutes or until a toothpick inserted near the center comes out clean. Cool for 10 minutes before removing from pans to a wire rack to cool completely.

In a small microwave-safe bowl, melt butter; add milk and baking cocoa. Microwave on high for 30 seconds. Whisk in confectioners' sugar and vanilla until smooth. Spread over the cakes. Sprinkle with chopped pecans if desired. **yield: 4 servings.**

Editor's Note: This recipe was tested in a 1,100-watt microwave.

tiny texas sheet cakes

classic cheesecake

Therese Fortier • *Grand Rapids, Michigan*
This simplicity of this cheesecake is what makes it so wonderful. Sometimes, I top each piece with fresh berries.

- 1/4 cup graham cracker crumbs
- 1 teaspoon sugar
- 4-1/2 teaspoons butter, melted

FILLING:
- 1 package (3 ounces) cream cheese, softened
- 1/4 cup sugar
- 1 egg, lightly beaten
- 1 teaspoon lemon juice
- 1/2 teaspoon grated lemon peel

TOPPING:
- 1/4 cup sour cream
- 2 teaspoons sugar
- 1/4 teaspoon vanilla extract

In a small bowl, combine cracker crumbs and sugar; stir in butter. Press onto the bottom of a greased 4-in. springform pan. Place on a baking sheet. Bake at 350° for 5 minutes. Cool on a wire rack.

In a small bowl, beat cream cheese and sugar until smooth. Add egg; beat on low speed just until combined. Stir in lemon juice and peel. Pour over crust. Return pan to baking sheet. Bake at 350° for 25-30 minutes or until center is almost set. Remove from oven; let stand 5 minutes (leave oven on).

Combine topping ingredients; carefully spread over filling. Bake 5 minutes longer. Cool on a wire rack for 10 minutes. Carefully run a knife around edge of pan to loosen; cool 1 hour longer. Refrigerate overnight. Remove sides of pan before serving. **yield: 2 servings.**

classic cheesecake

chocolate-almond banana splits

chocolate-almond banana splits

Candy McMenamin • *Lexington, South Carolina*
When your kids just can't wait to dig into something sweet, put together these speedy banana splits.

- 2 milk chocolate candy bars with almonds (1.45 ounces *each*), chopped
- 3 tablespoons heavy whipping cream
- 2 medium bananas
- 1 cup chocolate ice cream
- 2 tablespoons chopped almonds, toasted

In microwave, melt candy bars with cream. Stir until blended; keep warm. Halve bananas lengthwise; arrange in two dessert dishes. Add ice cream; drizzle with chocolate. Sprinkle with almonds. **yield: 2 servings.**

apple granola dessert

Janis Lawrence • *Childress, Texas*
My slow cooker makes simmering up this autumn treat a snap. Granola adds delicious texture.

- 4 medium tart apples, peeled and sliced
- 2 cups granola cereal with fruit and nuts
- 1/4 cup honey
- 2 tablespoons butter, melted
- 1 teaspoon ground cinnamon
- 1/2 teaspoon ground nutmeg
- Whipped topping, optional

In a 1-1/2-qt. slow cooker, combine apples and cereal. In a small bowl, combine the honey, butter, cinnamon and nutmeg; pour over apple mixture and mix well. Cover and cook on low for 6-8 hours. Serve with whipped topping if desired. **yield: 4-6 servings.**

chocolate panini

Kayla Wilcoxson, Abilene, Texas
I created this chocolaty sensation when I was learning to use my new panini maker. Sometimes I'll use different fruits…but the strawberry seems to be the favorite.

- 2 teaspoons butter, softened
- 2 slices white bread
- 1/2 teaspoon sugar
- 1 tablespoon cream cheese, softened
- 1/2 milk chocolate candy bar (1.55 ounces)
- 1/2 cup sliced fresh strawberries
- 1/4 cup heavy whipping cream, whipped

Butter one side of each slice of bread; sprinkle with sugar. Spread cream cheese over the other side. Place candy bar on the cream cheese side of one slice; top with the other slice, butter side up.

Cook on an indoor grill or panini maker for 2-3 minutes or until bread is browned and candy bar is melted. Cut in half; top with strawberries and whipped cream. **yield: 2 servings.**

cappuccino mousse

Taste of Home Test Kitchen
Our home economists dreamed up this silky mousse, which has a hint of coffee and a pleasantly creamy texture. Make it ahead for a delightful finale.

- 1/2 teaspoon unflavored gelatin
- 1/4 cup fat-free milk
- 1-1/2 teaspoons baking cocoa
- 1/4 teaspoon instant coffee granules
- 1/3 cup fat-free coffee-flavored yogurt
- 2 tablespoons sugar
- 1/2 cup reduced-fat whipped topping

In a small saucepan, sprinkle gelatin over milk; let stand for 1 minute. Heat over low heat, stirring until gelatin is completely dissolved. Add cocoa and coffee; stir until dissolved. Transfer to a small bowl; refrigerate until mixture begins to thicken.

Beat until light and fluffy. Combine yogurt and sugar; beat into gelatin mixture. Fold in whipping topping. Divide between two dessert dishes. Refrigerate mousse until firm. **yield: 2 servings.**

turtle cheesecake

turtle cheesecake

Erin Byrd • Springfield, Missouri
I always get compliments when I make this rich dessert. With layers of vanilla and fudge cream cheese plus a drizzle of caramel, this luscious cheesecake will win praise for you, too!

- 1/3 cup crushed vanilla wafers (about 10 wafers)
- 4 teaspoons butter, melted
- 4 ounces cream cheese, softened
- 2 tablespoons sugar
- 1/2 teaspoon vanilla extract
- 2 tablespoons beaten egg
- 2 tablespoons hot fudge ice cream topping, warmed
- 1 tablespoon caramel ice cream topping, warmed

In a small bowl, combine wafer crumbs and butter. Press onto the bottom and 1/2 in. up the sides of a greased 4-in. springform pan.

In a small bowl, beat the cream cheese, sugar and vanilla until smooth. Add egg; beat on low speed just until combined. Transfer half of the mixture to another bowl; stir in fudge topping. Pour remaining cream cheese mixture into crust. Top with chocolate mixture. Place pan on a baking sheet.

Bake at 350° for 20-25 minutes or until center is almost set. Cool on a wire rack for 10 minutes. Carefully run a knife around the edge of pan to loosen; cool 1 hour longer.

Refrigerate overnight. Drizzle caramel topping over cheesecake. Refrigerate leftovers. **yield: 2 servings.**

Lois Bayliff
Findlay, Ohio

This coconut cutie has a fluffy meringue filling that bakes to beautiful, tall peaks and is sprinkled with toasted coconut flakes.

coconut meringue pie

1/2   **cup all-purpose flour**
1/8   **teaspoon salt**
  2   **tablespoons shortening**
  2   **tablespoons cold water**
FILLING:
  3   **tablespoons sugar**
4-1/2   **teaspoons cornstarch**
  1   **cup 2% milk**
  2   **egg yolks**
  3   **tablespoons flaked coconut**
  1   **tablespoon butter**
MERINGUE:
  1   **egg white**
1/8   **teaspoon cream of tartar**
  2   **tablespoons sugar**
Flaked coconut, toasted, optional

In a small bowl, combine flour and salt; cut in shortening until crumbly. Gradually add water, tossing with a fork until dough forms a ball. Cover and refrigerate for 15 minutes or until easy to handle.

On a lightly floured surface, roll out pastry to fit a 5-in. pie plate. Transfer to pie plate. Trim to 1/2 in. beyond edge of plate; flute edges. Line unpricked pastry shell with a double thickness of heavy-duty foil. Bake at 450° for 5 minutes. Remove foil; bake 5 minutes longer. Cool on a wire rack.

For filling, in a small saucepan, combine the sugar, cornstarch, milk and egg yolks. Cook and stir over medium heat until mixture reaches 160° or is thick enough to coat the back of a metal spoon. Remove from the heat. Gently stir in coconut and butter. Pour into crust.

For meringue, in a small bowl, beat egg white and cream of tartar on medium speed until soft peaks form. Gradually beat in sugar, 1 tablespoon at a time, on high until stiff glossy peaks form and sugar is dissolved. Spread evenly over hot filling, sealing edges to crust.

Bake at 350° for 10-15 minutes or until meringue is golden brown. Cool on a wire rack for 30 minutes. Refrigerate for at least 3 hours before serving. Add flaked coconut if desired. **yield: 2 servings.**

hazelnut cheesecake parfaits

Shelly Platten • Amherst, Wisconsin

These parfaits are as delicious as they are eye-catching! Guests will be delighted to see these on your dinner table.

- 1/4 cup chopped hazelnuts
- 1/2 teaspoon sugar
- 1/3 cup semisweet chocolate chips
- 2 tablespoons half-and-half cream
- 2 tablespoons whipped cream cheese
- 2 teaspoons brown sugar
- 1/2 cup coffee yogurt
- 1/4 teaspoon vanilla extract
- 2/3 cup whipped topping
- 2 whole chocolate graham crackers, crushed

Chocolate curls and additional whipped topping, optional

In a small heavy skillet, cook and stir the hazelnuts over medium heat until toasted, about 4 minutes. Sprinkle with sugar; cook and stir for 2-4 minutes or until sugar is melted. Spread on foil to cool.

In a small saucepan, melt chocolate chips with cream over low heat; stir until smooth. Remove from the heat; cool to room temperature. In a small bowl, beat cream cheese and brown sugar until blended. Beat in yogurt and vanilla; fold in whipped topping.

In two parfait glasses, layer the graham crackers, yogurt mixture, chocolate mixture and hazelnuts. Refrigerate until chilled. Garnish with chocolate curls and whipped topping if desired. **yield: 2 servings.**

hazelnut cheesecake parfaits

almond chocolate cakes

almond chocolate cakes

Mary Lou Wayman • Salt Lake City, Utah

I serve this variation of chocolate cake often, and it is always a hit. It is almost like a steamed pudding, served warm and topped with whipped cream or ice cream. The chocolate-praline flavor comes through nicely in every bite.

- 1/3 cup packed brown sugar
- 2 tablespoons butter, melted
- 2 tablespoons half-and-half cream
- 1/4 cup finely chopped almonds

BATTER:

- 1/2 cup sugar
- 2 tablespoons butter, softened
- 1 egg
- 1/4 teaspoon vanilla extract
- 1/2 cup all-purpose flour
- 2 tablespoons baking cocoa
- 1/2 teaspoon baking powder
- 1/4 teaspoon baking soda
- 1/3 cup milk

Combine the brown sugar, butter and cream; divide between two greased 10-oz. ramekins or custard cups. Sprinkle with almonds.

In a small bowl, beat sugar and butter until crumbly, about 2 minutes. Beat in egg and vanilla. Combine the flour, cocoa, baking powder and baking soda; add to sugar mixture alternately with milk, beating well after each addition. Divide between ramekins. Place on a baking sheet.

Bake at 350° for 20-25 minutes or until a toothpick inserted near the center comes out clean. Cool for 5 minutes before inverting onto plates. Serve warm. **yield: 2 servings.**

General Recipe Index

This index lists every recipe by food category and/or major ingredient,
so you can easily locate recipes to suit your needs. An alphabetical index begins on page 111.

Onion Soup with Sausage, 42
Salisbury Steak with Portobello
    Sauce, 88

Nuts & Peanut Butter
Almond Cheese Spread, 29
Almond Chocolate Cakes, 107
Butter Pecan French Toast, 16
Chocolate-Almond Banana
    Splits, 104
Five-Spiced Pecans, 23
Fudgy Peanut Butter Cake, 99
Hazelnut Cheesecake Parfaits, 107
Nutty Salmon, 86
PBJ-Stuffed French Toast, 12
Pecan Cheddar Snacks, 35
Pine Nut-Crusted Tilapia, 76
Pistachio Cranberry Orzo, 69
Pork with Apples 'n' Hazelnuts, 74
Pumpkin Waffles with Orange
    Walnut Butter, 11
Roasted Pears in Pecan Sauce, 93
Thai Shrimp Linguine, 76
Walnut Rice, 67

Oats & Granola
Apple Granola Dessert, 104
Blueberry Crumble, 102
Cranberry Oat Bread, 58
Honey Oatmeal Bread, 66
Oh-So-Good Oatmeal, 13
Grilled Peach Crisps for 2, 93
Rhubarb Crisp, 98

Onions & Green Onions
Cheesy Onion Biscuits, 55
Chunky Bloody Mary Salsa, 29
Fried Onion Rings, 29
Deep-Fried Onions with Dipping
    Sauce, 27
Onion au Gratin, 62
Onion Soup with Sausage, 42

Oranges
Gingered Orange Beets, 60
Honey-Orange Chicken Wings, 36
Mandarin Chicken Coleslaw, 58
Orange Pork Chops, 82
Pumpkin Waffles with Orange
    Walnut Butter, 11
Spinach Salad with Curry
    Dressing, 59

Pancakes, Crepes, French Toast & Waffles
Apple Pancakes with Cider Syrup, 5
Blueberry Cheesecake Flapjacks, 6
Butter Pecan French Toast, 16

Chicken Broccoli Crepes, 8
Cottage Cheese Waffles, 7
Ham 'n' Cheese Crepes, 17
Multigrain Pancakes, 10
PBJ-Stuffed French Toast, 12
Puffy Oven Pancakes, 14
Pumpkin Waffles with Orange
    Walnut Butter, 11
Raspberry French Toast Cups, 18

Pasta & Couscous
Apricot Chicken Pasta, 87
Asian Shrimp Soup, 53
Couscous with Mushrooms, 70
Creamy Spring Soup, 40
Fettuccine with Green
    Vegetables, 63
Garlic-Herb Orzo Pilaf, 56
Lemon Chicken with Pasta, 83
Pasta with Sausage 'n' Peppers, 85
Pistachio Cranberry Orzo, 69
Seafood Fettuccine Alfredo, 77
Simple Minestrone, 41
Toasted Ravioli, 23

Pastrami, Pepperoni & Salami
Garden Fresh Subs, 47
Pepperoni Roll-Ups, 24
Spinach Pastrami Wraps, 42

Peaches & Pears
Glazed Ham with Sweet
    Potatoes, 80
Grilled Peach Crisps for 2, 93
Peachy Sweet Potatoes, 62
Roasted Pears in Pecan Sauce, 93

Peppers
Bacon Jalapeno Poppers, 27
Grilled Cheese & Pepper
    Sandwiches, 52
Grilled Pepper Jack Chicken
    Sandwiches, 43
Hot 'n' Spicy Cranberry Dip, 30
Pasta with Sausage 'n' Peppers, 85
Roasted Pepper, Bacon & Egg
    Muffins, 9
Santa Fe Deviled Eggs, 33

Pork
Cheesy Tenderloin Strips, 37
Cranberry Pork Tenderloin, 86
Indonesian Pork, 81
Orange Pork Chops, 82
Pork with Apples 'n' Hazelnuts, 74
Swedish Meatballs, 87

Potatoes & Sweet Potatoes
Autumn Chowder, 52
Brunch Egg Burritos, 15
Buttery Garlic Potatoes, 58
Cordon Bleu Potato Soup, 52
Glazed Ham with Sweet
    Potatoes, 80
Grilled Potato Skins, 26
Hash Brown Breakfast
    Casserole, 16
Hearty Breakfast Combo, 7
Hearty Cheese Soup, 43
Hearty Chicken-Filled Potato, 89
Microwave Potato Chips, 28
Peachy Sweet Potatoes, 62
Potato Chip Chicken Strips, 35
Potato Vegetable Soup, 47
Sweet Potato Fries, 67
Twice-Baked Deviled Potatoes, 64

Pumpkin
Gingered Pumpkin Bisque, 48
Maple Pumpkin Pie, 92
Pumpkin Waffles with Orange
    Walnut Butter, 11

Quick Breads
Buttery Sour Cream Muffins, 64
Cheesy Onion Biscuits, 55
Cranberry Scones, 71
Ginger Currant Scones, 63
Whole Wheat Biscuits, 57

Rice & Quinoa
Creamy Wild Rice Soup, 50
Garlic-Herb Orzo Pilaf, 56
Quinoa Pilaf, 59
Sausage Rice Casserole, 80
Walnut Rice, 67

Sausage
Hearty Breakfast Combo, 7
Onion Soup with Sausage, 42
Pasta with Sausage 'n' Peppers, 85
Sausage Cheese Balls, 33
Sausage Rice Casserole, 80

Spinach
Beefstro Bruschetta Burgers, 46
Bistro Breakfast Panini, 17
Creamy Spring Soup, 40
Phyllo-Wrapped Halibut, 84
Spinach Cheese Soup, 50
Spinach Pastrami Wraps, 42
Spinach Salad with Curry
    Dressing, 59

Alphabetic Index